GUIDE TO PANELING AND WALLBOARD

McGraw-Hill Paperbacks
Home Improvement Series

GUIDE TO PANELING AND WALLBOARD

McGRAW-HILL BOOK COMPANY

New York   St. Louis   San Francisco   Auckland   Bogotá   Düsseldorf
Johannesburg   London   Madrid   Mexico   Montreal   New Delhi   Panama
Paris   São Paulo   Singapore   Sydney   Tokyo   Toronto

1 2 3 4 5 6 7 8 9 0 SMSM 8 3 2 1 0

Library of Congress Cataloging in Publication Data
Main entry under title:

Guide to paneling and wallboard.

  (McGraw-Hill paperbacks home improvement series)
  Originally issued in 1975 by the Automotive-
Hardware Trades Division of the Minnesota Mining and
Manufacturing Company under title: The home pro
paneling and wallboard guide.
    1. Paneling—Amateurs' manual. 2. Wall board—
Amateurs' manuals. I. Minnesota Mining and
Manufacturing Company. Automotive-Hardware Trades
Division. The home pro paneling and wallboard guide.
TH8581.M56 1980   698   79-13991
ISBN 0-07-045963-0

Front cover photo courtesy of Champion Building Products,
Champion International Corporation, Stamford,
Connecticut.

Back cover photos courtesy of Georgia-Pacific Corporation,
Portland, Oregon.

Contents

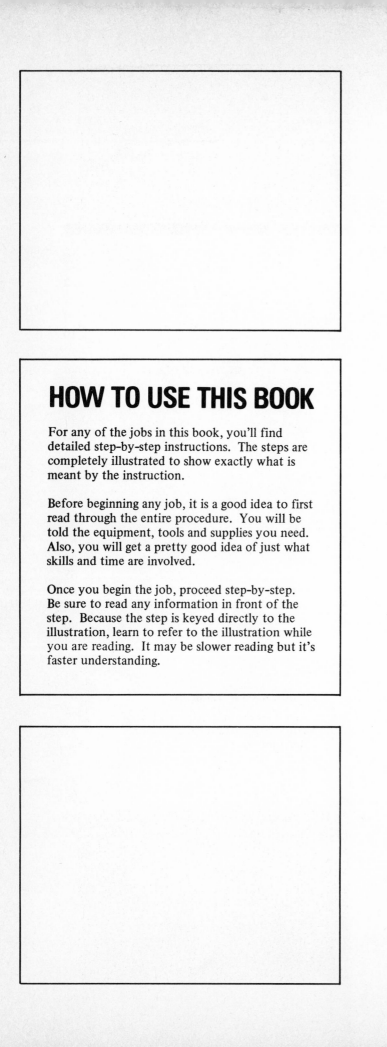

HOW TO USE THIS BOOK

For any of the jobs in this book, you'll find detailed step-by-step instructions. The steps are completely illustrated to show exactly what is meant by the instruction.

Before beginning any job, it is a good idea to first read through the entire procedure. You will be told the equipment, tools and supplies you need. Also, you will get a pretty good idea of just what skills and time are involved.

Once you begin the job, proceed step-by-step. Be sure to read any information in front of the step. Because the step is keyed directly to the illustration, learn to refer to the illustration while you are reading. It may be slower reading but it's faster understanding.

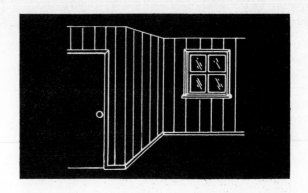

WOOD PANELING

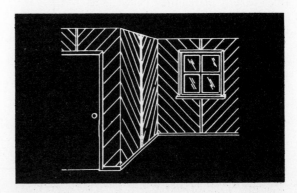

The three kinds of wood paneling which are commonly used for decorative paneling are

Veneered plywood sheet panels, Page 2.
Coated hardboard sheet panels, Page 7.
Solid board panels, Page 7.

▶ **Veneered Plywood Sheet Panels**

Plywood panels are made of thin sheets of wood [1] held together with moisture resistant glue. On decorative panels, a very thin layer of hardwood [2] is glued onto the face of the panel. This layer is called a veneer. Woods such as oak, walnut and mahogany are used for veneers.

In recent years, simulated veneers have become increasingly popular. A wide variety of wood grains and colors is chemically produced on inexpensive woods. Excellent reproductions of expensive hardwoods are available as well as unusual and interesting decorative effects.

Panels are ordinarily available in 4 foot by 8 foot sheets. However, some can be ordered in lengths up to 16 feet. Decorative panels most commonly range in thicknesss from 3/16-inch to 3/8-inch.

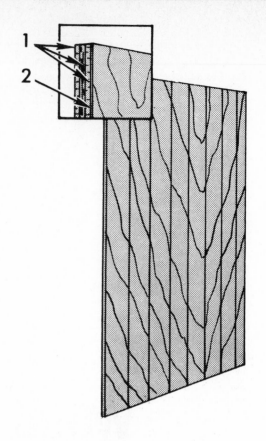

Veneered Plywood Sheet Panels

There is a large variety of molding and trim on the market. Much of it is designed especially for use with plywood paneling. Common materials for molding and trim are wood, aluminum and vinyl.

Aluminum and vinyl moldings are generally designed to be installed before the panels. The panels are then slipped into place against the molding. Examples of these moldings are shown in the illustration. Typical wood moldings are also shown to illustrate the differences between them regarding installation procedures.

Many panel manufacturers produce molding with finishes which exactly match their panels. Prefinished molding has the advantage of convenience but is more expensive than unfinished wood molding. Unfinished wood molding can be stained to closely match panel finishes or painted in contrasting colors.

All molding, regardless of material, has two purposes:

- It provides a finished professional appearance to the paneling job.

- It covers gaps between the different surfaces. The measurement and cutting of panels can thus proceed much faster if molding is used since the fitting of panels need not be so precise.

Molding is made for use at ceilings, corners, floors, around windows and doors, and at edges of enclosures or other obstructions.

Material	Inside Corner	Outside Corner	Seam	Cap
Aluminum				
Vinyl				
Wood				

Veneered Plywood Sheet Panels

The use of molding is partly a matter of individual preference and partly a matter of convenience. Considerations in the application of molding are discussed in the following paragraphs. The descriptions are limited to conventional wood molding.

● Ceilings. Whether or not to use molding between the ceiling and walls depends upon personal preference. If molding is not used, considerable cutting to fit the panel to the ceiling may be required. The line between the ceiling and walls is often quite uneven and this fact becomes apparent when the panel is placed against it.

A special molding called cove molding [1] is made to conceal the gap between the ceiling and walls. Cove molding is made in different sizes [2] and styles [3] to accommodate almost any decorating need.

Quarter round molding [4] or shoe molding [5] should not be used in place of cove molding between the ceiling and walls. The corners [6] of the molding may interfere with obtaining a good fit between the ceiling and walls.

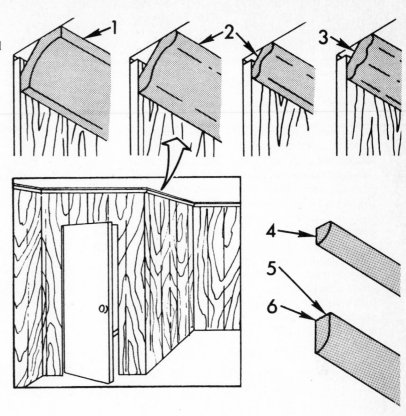

Veneered Plywood Sheet Panels

In situations where the tops of the panels do not meet the ceiling [1] or where panels are used for wainscoting [2], a special molding designed to conceal the edges of panels is used. This molding is called cap molding [3].

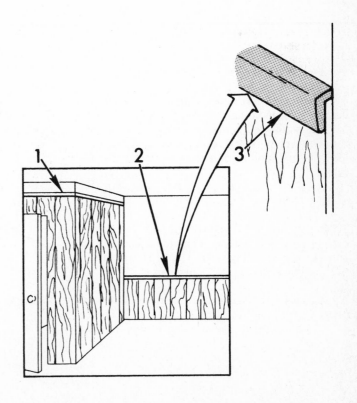

3

Veneered Plywood Sheet Panels

● Corners. Outside corners are trimmed with molding called outside corner molding [1]. Outside corner molding is used on outside corners of column enclosures [2] as well as wall corners. In some cases, it may be used to trim corners formed between casement windows and walls.

The alternative to using molding at corners is to join the edges of panels at corners with miter joints [3]. Corners in rooms are, however, seldom straight enough to permit a good-fitting miter joint. The precision of measuring, cutting and fitting a miter joint in this application is exacting. Therefore, corner molding is generally recommended for outside corners.

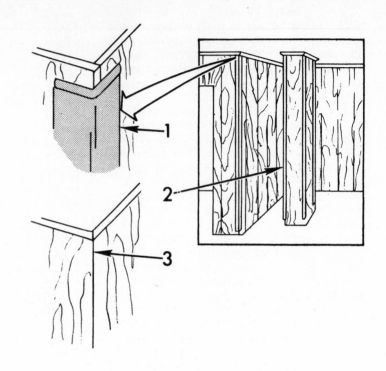

Veneered Plywood Sheet Panels

Inside corners are trimmed with molding called inside corner molding [1]. Most corners formed between walls are uneven. There will generally be gaps between plywood panels meeting at corners. Inside corner molding is designed to conceal these gaps.

Quarter round molding [2] or shoe molding [3] should not be used in place of inside corner molding at inside corners. The corners [4] of these moldings will interfere with obtaining a good fit between the adjoining walls. Gaps [5] between the molding and the panel will occur.

An alternative to using inside corner molding is to precisely trim the panels which meet at the corner so that no noticeable gap appears between them.

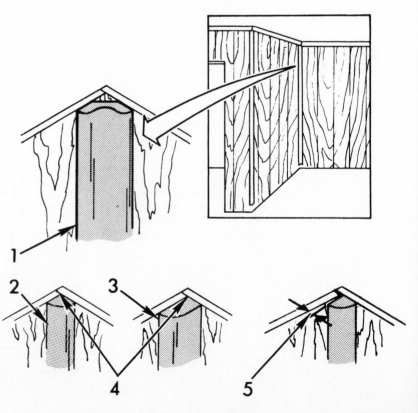

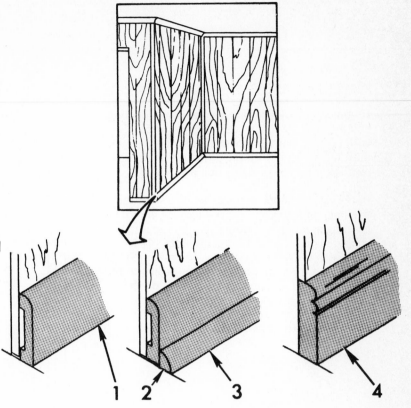

Veneered Plywood Sheet Panels

● Floors. If a room is going to be finished with wall-to-wall carpeting, it is not necessary to use base molding [1]. The carpeting will conceal the gap between the bottom of the panel and the floor. However, many persons prefer to use base molding in all cases. It protects the bottom of the panel from damage from sweepers, toys or other abuse.

Base molding [1] can be used alone or in combination with shoe molding [2]. Shoe molding [2] may be necessary to conceal a gap [3] between base molding and tile or other floor covering.

If the room already has a thick enough baseboard [4], it may be possible to simply trim and butt the panel to fit against the baseboard.

Veneered Plywood Sheet Panels

● Doors and Windows. The most difficult trimming problems are presented by windows and doors. The following paragraphs provide several solutions — one of which may be the best solution for your particular situation.

If you have thick enough window and door moldings [1], it may be possible to simply fit and butt [2] the panels against the existing moldings.

If your existing molding is the style illustrated [3], you may wish to reuse it. An exact cutout for the plywood can be made in the molding [3] with a dado [5]. Using a bench saw with a dado setup, cut a 1/4-inch rabbet [4] as shown. Be sure to measure and trim the panel so that its edge will be concealed by the molding.

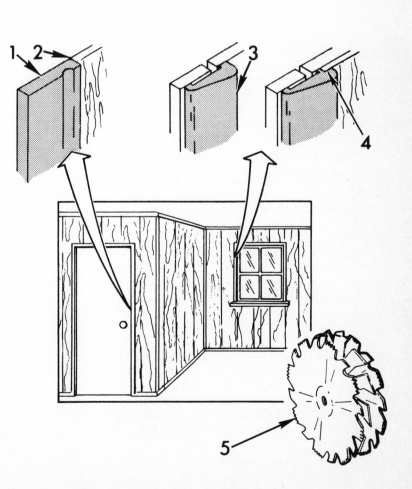

5

Veneered Plywood Sheet Panels

If you do not wish to save your existing molding, you may choose to conceal the edges of panels with cap molding [2]. Note that in this case you must measure and trim the panel so that the edge overlaps the window frame or door frame [1].

In the case of doors, you may wish to solve the trimming problem by "concealing" the door itself. Existing molding is removed and the panel [5] is measured and trimmed so that its edge [4] is flush with the door frame [3]. The piece [6] that is removed from the panel is then attached to the door. This will ensure that the pattern on the door matches the pattern on the wall. The door will appear to be part of the wall. The visual effect will be to make the room look larger.

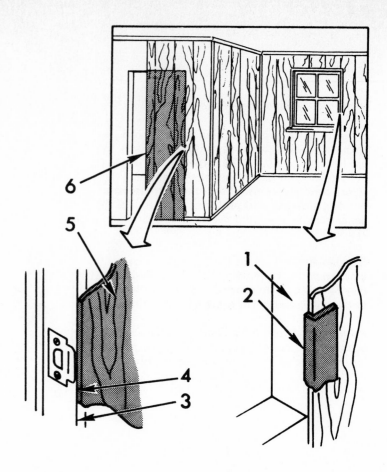

Veneered Plywood Sheet Panels

• Seams. The seams between adjoining veneered plywood panels are seldom covered with molding. The wood grain patterns and the simulated planking combine to make seams almost invisible.

To prevent the wall from showing at seams, paint the strip of wall behind the seam black or cover it with a strip of black plastic tape.

However, if it is necessary or preferable to cover the seams, a special seam molding [1] is available.

• Other Molding and Trim. Other molding and trim which may be required to complete the paneling job are:

Window mullions [2]
Window sills [3] and stools [4]
Door stops [5]

These items are available in unfinished and pre-finished form. Unfinished material is usually soft pine or fir which may be stained to match the panels.

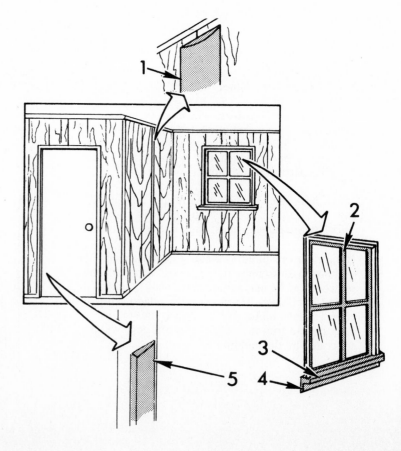

▶ Coated Hardboard Sheet Panels

Hardboard panels are made by compressing wood pulp and fibers into sheets. These sheets are then given a decorative surface. The most common decorative panels are enameled or plastic laminated. A large variety of colors and patterns is produced.

Hardboard panels are ordinarily available in 4 foot by 8 foot sheets but can be ordered in 16 foot lengths. The most common thicknesses for these panels are 1/8-inch and 1/4-inch.

Special trim and molding are made for hardboard panels. They are available in matching or contrasting finishes.

Molding for hardboard panels is attached to the wall before the panel is installed. The panel is then slid into place in the molding. There are four kinds of molding used with hardboard panels:

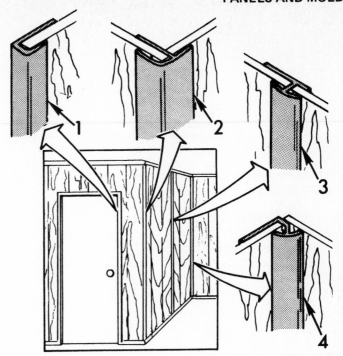

Cap molding [1]. Used at exposed edges of panels including ceilings, wainscoting, doors and windows.

Outside corner molding [2]. Used at outside corners.

Seam or divider bar molding [3]. Used at vertical seams between adjoining panels.

Inside corner molding [4]. Used at inside corners.

▶ Solid Board Panels

Solid board panels are available in hardwoods or softwoods. They are produced in rough or smooth finishes and clear or knotty grades.

The thickness of boards used for interior decorating commonly varies from 1/2-inch to 7/8-inch. They are obtainable in almost any length.

Widths of boards range from 3 inches to 12 inches. Decorators will sometimes use a variety of widths to panel a room. Interesting visual effects can be achieved by randomly installing different widths of boards. In fact, many sheet panels are made to simulate random width planks.

Three different types of edges are commonly used for joining these boards:

Tongue in groove [1]
Shiplap [2]
Square edge [3]

Shiplap joints and tongue in groove joints are interlocking. Square edge joints can simply butt against each other [4]. To obtain interesting effects, however, board on board [5] or batten on board [6] joints can be used.

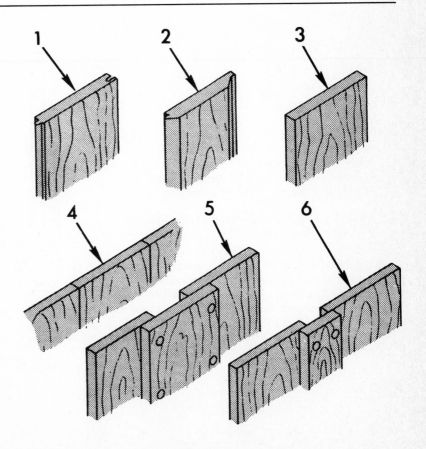

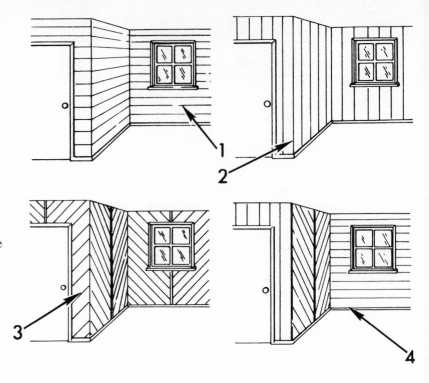

Solid Board Panels

Other interesting effects can be obtained by installing the boards to form:

> Horizontal patterns [1]
> Vertical patterns [2]
> Herringbone patterns [3]

These patterns may be used together in the same room to produce visual interest [4].

Solid Board Panels

Molding is generally used at the ceiling, around columns, beams and cupboards, and around windows and doors. The use of molding at the floor is optional. If wall-to-wall carpeting is to be installed, base molding is often omitted.

There is a large variety of molding patterns and sizes to choose from. Selection of molding styles and methods of trimming are a matter of personal preference. In general, however, base molding [1] should be used at the floor, casing molding [3] should be used around windows and doors, and crown molding [2] should be used at the ceiling. Quarter round molding [4] and other trim molding [5] is often used for covering gaps between panels and obstructions.

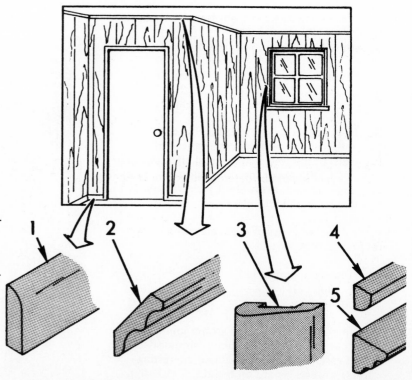

▶ Estimating Sheet or Solid Board Paneling

Before the number of sheets or boards needed can be determined, the width of sheets or boards must be known.

Be sure the length of the sheets or boards is equal to, or greater than, the height of the wall.

1. Measure and record width of all surfaces to be paneled.

2. Divide width recorded in Step 1 by the width of one sheet or board. Increase number to next higher whole number. If using sheets, add widths of all surfaces to be paneled before calculating number of sheets.

3. Determine areas of all surfaces which are not to be paneled. Add all areas and record total.

4. Divide total area recorded in Step 3 by area of one board or panel. Record lowest whole number.

5. Subtract result of Step 4 from result of Step 2 to determine number of sheets or boards required to panel surfaces.

▶ Estimating Molding and Baseboards

Molding and baseboard are sold by the foot. To determine how many feet you need, measure and record lengths along which molding or baseboard is to be installed.

1. Determine specific kind of molding (cap, crown, casing, etc.) required for each application.

2. For each type of molding, determine number of feet required. Increase fractions to next higher foot.

To avoid splicing short pieces of molding, it may be necessary to purchase extra lengths of molding.

ARRANGING VENEERED PLYWOOD SHEET PANELS FOR GRAIN AND COLOR

Unless simulated wood grain veneers are used, grain pattern and color will be different for each panel.

The arrangement of panels which gives the best appearance should be determined before beginning installation.

1. Arrange panels [1] against wall at desired position. Rearrange panels to give best appearance.

2. Number the back of each panel [1] in the order that panels are to be installed.

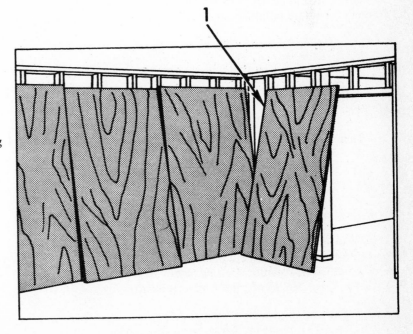

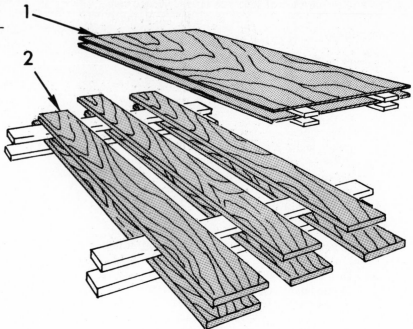

Panels expand or contract according to temperature and moisture conditions of surrounding air. Therefore, they should be stored for at least 48 hours in the room to be paneled before installation.

If the room is damp from wet plaster or concrete, it must be allowed to dry thoroughly before installing panels.

Panels may be conditioned by placing them around the room so that air can circulate freely around them. If they cannot be placed around the room, stack them as follows:

- Sheet panels [1] should be stacked so that each panel is separated from the next by two furring strips.

- Boards [2] should be stacked so that each board is separated from the next by two furring strips.

PREPARATION FOR PANELING

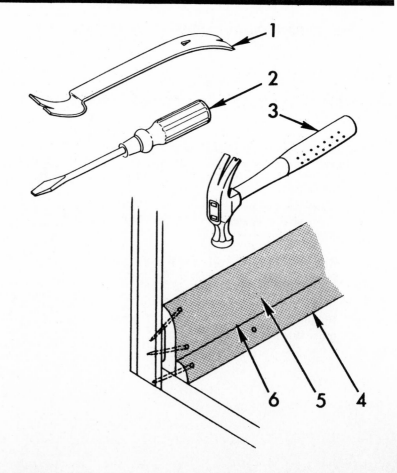

▶ **Removing Baseboards and Molding**

Unless you plan to butt panels against existing baseboards and molding, these items must be removed before installing panels.

The following tools and supplies are required:

Pry bar [1] or long screwdriver [2]
Claw hammer [3]
Pieces of scrap wood

If you work carefully, you may be able to salvage existing material for reuse.

If shoe molding [4] is installed, it must be removed. Go to Step 1.

If shoe molding is not installed, go to Step 5.

1. If shoe molding [4] and baseboard [5] have been painted, first cut paint along joint [6] with a sharp knife. Cutting paint will prevent uneven peeling of paint from baseboard.

2. Starting at one end of shoe molding strip [4], insert pry bar between shoe molding [4] and baseboard [5].

Removing Baseboards and Molding

3. Place piece of wood [1] between pry bar and baseboard to prevent damaging baseboard.

4. Carefully pry shoe molding away from baseboard.

5. Starting at one end of baseboard [2], insert pry bar between baseboard and wall.

6. Carefully pry baseboard away from wall.

7. Starting at one end of casing molding [3], insert pry bar between molding and wall.

8. Carefully pry casing molding away from wall and frame [4].

9. Using hammer and block of wood [5], remove nails from molding and walls. If nails are difficult to remove from wall, hammer them flush with wall.

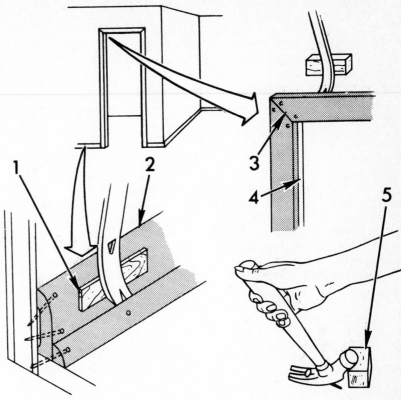

▶ **Locating and Marking Studs**

If you are installing hardboard panels [2] on sound even walls, it is not necessary to locate studs. Molding [1] is fastened to wall where needed with adhesive and panels [2] are secured to molding and walls.

If you are installing veneered plywood sheet panels [3], locate and mark each stud on which a panel edge [4] will be placed. Mark stud with a plumb line to aid in aligning panel vertically. Locate and mark these studs even if you are planning to install panels with adhesive rather than nails. Edges of panels may eventually pull away from wall and require nailing at a later time.

If you are installing furring strips [5] on the wall, locate and mark each stud.

If you are installing solid board panels in a horizontal pattern [6] or a diagonal or herringbone pattern [7], locate and mark each stud.

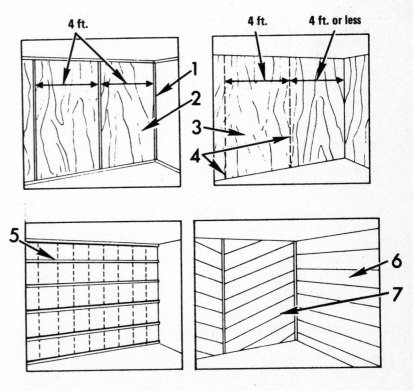

PREPARATION FOR PANELING

Locating and Marking Studs

Studs [3] are usually installed at intervals [2] of 16 inches but in some houses or some walls they may be installed at intervals of 20 or 24 inches.

Studs [3] can be located by one of the following methods:

- Hand or hammer method, Page 12.
- Nail or drill method , Page 12.
- Magnetic stud finder method , Page 13.

   A magnetic stud finder [1] is an inexpensive tool available at any hardware store. It consists of a holder and magnetic pointer which moves when it comes near metal such as the nails which hold wallboard to studs.

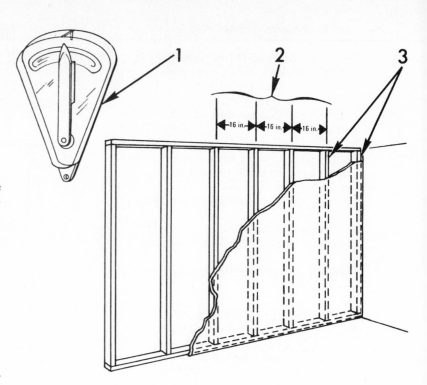

▶ **Locating Studs — Hand or Hammer Method**

Begin locating studs [3] at one corner and work from there around entire room.

1.   Using fist or hammer, firmly tap wall.

If solid sound is heard, stud [3] is behind surface. Go to Step 2.

If hollow sound is heard, stud [3] is not behind surface. Repeat Step 1 until solid sound is heard.

Locating and Marking Studs — Hand or Hammer Method

2.   Place a mark [2] near ceiling at location of stud [1].

3.   Measure 16 inches, 20 inches, or 24 inches horizontally from mark [2]. Repeat Steps 1 and 2.

Note distance at which next stud [1] is found. Look for further studs at intervals of that distance.

4.   Repeat Steps 1 through 3 until all required studs [1] are located.

5.   Mark each stud with a vertical line from ceiling to floor. If stud should be marked with a plumb line , go to Page 13 for marking a plumb line.

▶ **Locating Studs — Nail or Drill Method**

Begin locating studs [1] at one corner and work from there around entire room.

1.   Using hammer and nail or drill and bit, make a hole in surface.

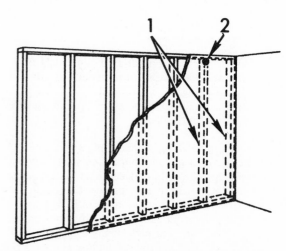

If nail or bit hits wood, stud [1] is behind surface. Go to Step 2.

If nail or bit does not hit wood, repeat Step 1 until nail or bit hits wood.

2.   Place a mark [2] near ceiling at location of stud [1].

3.   Measure 16 inches, 20 inches, or 24 inches horizontally from mark [2]. Repeat Steps 1 and 2.

Locating and Marking Studs — Nail or Drill Method

Note distance at which next stud [1] is found.
Look for further studs at intervals of that distance.

4. Repeat Steps 1 through 3 until all required
    studs [1] are located.

5. Mark each stud with a vertical line from
    ceiling to floor. If stud should be marked
    with a plumb line, go to lower half of page
    for marking a plumb line.

▶ **Locating and Marking Studs — Magnetic Stud
Finder Method**

Begin locating studs [1] at one corner and work
from there around entire room.

1. Following manufacturer's instructions, locate
    stud [1] with magnetic stud finder.

2. Place mark [2] near ceiling at location of
    stud [1].

3. Measure 16 inches, 20 inches or 24 inches
    horizontally from mark [2]. Repeat Steps 1
    and 2.

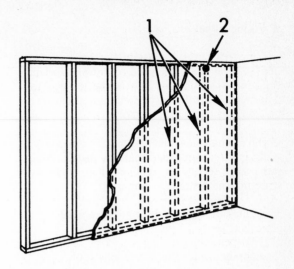

Note distance at which next stud [1] is found.
Look for further studs at intervals of that distance.

4. Repeat Steps 1 through 3 until all required
    studs [1] are located.

5. Mark each stud with a vertical line from
    ceiling to floor. If stud should be marked
    with a plumb line, go to next section (below)
    for marking a plumb line.

▶ **Locating and Marking Studs — Marking a Plumb
Line**

A plumb line is a line that is exactly vertical.
It can be determined and marked easily by use of
a chalked string and a plumb or other weight.

1. Place tack in mark [1] near ceiling. Tie
    string [2] to tack. Tie plumb [4] or other
    weight to string.

2. Release plumb [4]. When plumb stops
    swinging, place mark [3] on wall directly
    behind string.

3. Rub string with colored chalk.

4. While holding string [2] tightly between
    tack and mark, pull string straight back from
    wall. Release string.

Chalk will mark straight plumb line on wall.

5. Remove tack and string.

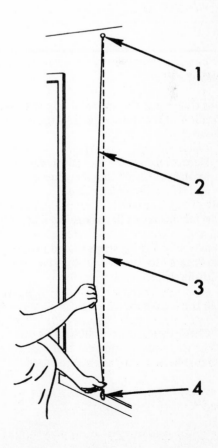

PREPARATION FOR PANELING

▶ Checking a Wall

Furring strips must be installed on walls that are uneven or in badly damaged condition. Instructions in this section tell how to check a wall to determine if furring strips are required before installing panels.

If you are paneling concrete block or masonry walls, it is recommended that you install framing rather than furring strips. Go to Page 18 for constructing and installing framing.

The following tools and supplies are needed:

> Carpenter's level [1]
> Straight 6 foot or 8 foot length of
>   2 in. x 4 in., or other straightedge

Carpenter's level is used to check if wall is plumb. Wall should be checked at several locations.

1. Place carpenter's level [1] against wall. Check that bubble [2] is in exact center of scale.

If bubble [2] is not in exact center of scale, wall is not plumb. Furring strips should be installed.

Go to Page 11 to locate wall studs before installing furring strips.

If wall is plumb, continue.

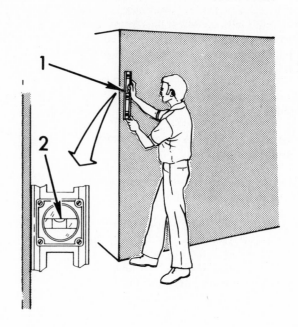

Checking a Wall

Wall is true if it is flat and level across its entire surface. Wall is not true if it has high or low spots on its surface.

2. Place straightedge [1] against wall at several locations. Check that straightedge is flat against wall at all locations.

If straightedge is not flat against wall at all locations, wall is not true. High or low spots should be removed or furring strips should be installed. Go to Page 11 to locate wall studs before installing furring strips.

If wall is true, continue.

3. Check that plaster, wallboard or other covering is in sound condition. All wall covering must be securely fastened to studs.

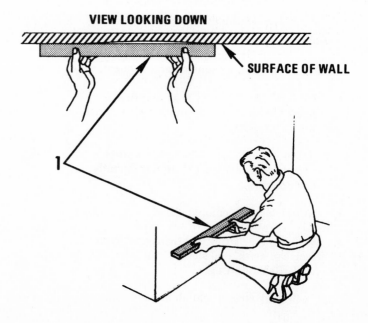

VIEW LOOKING DOWN

SURFACE OF WALL

▶ **Furring a Wall**

Furring strips are used to provide an even surface for installing panels. They are used to correct badly damaged or uneven walls.

Furring strips also provide a fastening surface for panels. For example, if you plan to install board panels [3] vertically over exposed studs [1], it is first necessary to construct a nailing surface with furring strips [2].

Remember that furring strips will increase the wall thickness by about one inch. Therefore, it will be necessary to move electrical switches and outlets the same distance. Also, door frames and window frames will require change. In general, furring strips must be installed around all door openings, window openings and other openings to provide a fastening surface for panels and wall mounted fixtures.

The following tools and supplies are required:

    Tape measure [4]
    Carpenter's level [5]
    Hammer [6]

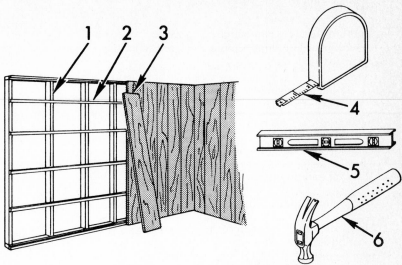

Common nails. 7 penny (2-1/4 inches) for nailing furring strips to exposed studs; 8 penny (2-1/2 inches) for nailing furring strips to studs covered by wallboard or plaster. If fastening furring strips to concrete block or masonry walls, use 4 penny (1-1/2 inches) masonry nails.
Shingles or scrap wood to be used for shims
1 in. x 2 in. furring strips

Furring a Wall

If you plan to install board panels in a horizontal pattern [1], furring strips should be installed vertically [2] to provide a good fastening surface. Go to Page 17 for installing furring strips vertically.

Furring strips should be installed horizontally [3] for all other paneling. Go to Step 1 for installing furring strips horizontally.

1.   Measure and record width of wall.

2.   Measure and cut strip [5] at width recorded in Step 1.

3.   Drive one nail [6] through each end of strip [5] until ends of nails just show.

First strip [7] is installed 1/4-inch above floor. Remaining strips are installed with their centers at 16 inch intervals [4].

4.   Place and hold strip [7] at installed position. Drive nail [6] into wall.

Strip is level when bubble [10] is in exact center of scale.

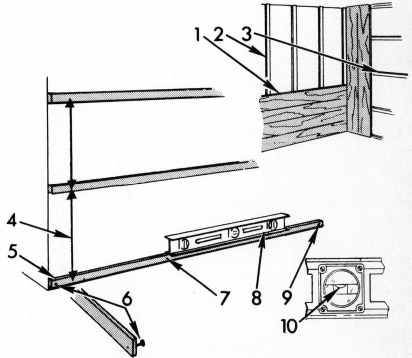

5.   Place carpenter's level [8] on top edge of strip [7]. Move strip up or down until bubble [10] is in exact center of scale.

6.   While holding strip [7] at level position, drive nail [9] into wall.

PREPARATION FOR PANELING

Furring a Wall

In following steps, straightedge is used to determine where shims should be placed to level furring strip.

7. Hold a straightedge [1] against wall 1/4-inch above strip [2].

8. Check that there are no gaps [3] between straightedge [1] and wall.

If no gaps are found, go to Step 11.

If gaps are found, continue.

Shims are placed between furring strip and wall at locations of gaps. Shims of different thicknesses may be needed.

9. Insert shims [5] behind strip [2] until inside surface of strip is even with inside surface of straightedge. Secure shim [5] by driving nail [4] through furring strip [2] and shim [5] and into wall.

10. Repeat Steps 7 through 9 for entire length of strip [2].

11. Nail furring strip [2] to wall at each stud.

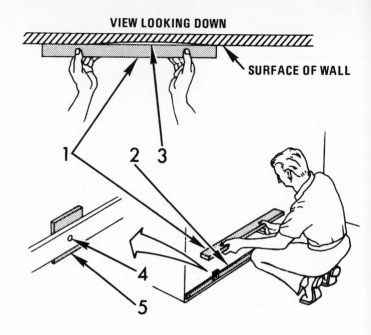

VIEW LOOKING DOWN

SURFACE OF WALL

12. Repeat Steps 2 through 11 to install and level remaining furring strips.

If solid board paneling is being installed, furring the wall is completed. If sheet paneling is being installed, continue.

Furring a Wall

Vertical strips must be installed between horizontal strips to provide additional support at edges of sheet panels.

13. Cut vertical strips into 13-inch lengths.

First vertical strip [1] is installed in a top corner. Second vertical strip [3] is located so that edge of panel [2] will be on center of strip [3]. Remaining strips [5] are installed with their centers at 48-inch intervals [4].

14. Drive one nail through each end of strip [9] until ends of nails just show.

Spaces [6] between vertical strips and horizontal strips are 1/2-inch. Spaces are required to permit ventilation.

15. Place vertical strip [1] at installed position.

16. While holding strip [1] at vertical position, drive top and bottom nails into wall.

17. Repeat Step 13 through Step 16 to install remaining vertical strips.

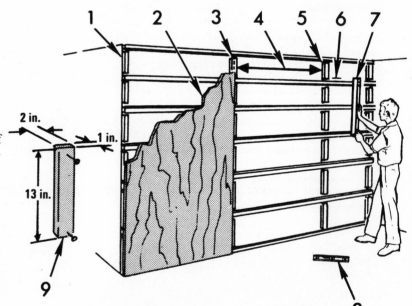

18. Place straightedge [7] on vertical strips. Check for gaps and shim strips as required.

19. Using carpenter's level [8], check that surface of wall is vertical. Shim strips as required.

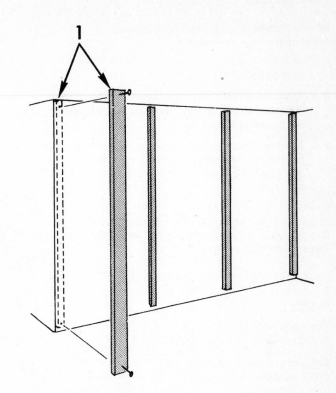

▶ **Furring a Wall for Horizontal Solid Board Panels**

1. Measure height of wall. Subtract 1 inch from height to allow for gap at top and bottom of furring strips.

2. Measure and cut strips at length determined in Step 1.

3. Drive one nail through each end of strip [1] until ends of nails just show.

First strip [1] is installed in a corner. Remaining strips are installed on alternate wall studs (32-inch intervals).

4. Place strip [1] at installed position. Drive top nail into wall or stud.

5. While aligning strip [1] on stud, drive bottom nail into wall or stud.

Furring a Wall for Horizontal Solid Board Panels

6. Place carpenter's level [3] on face of strip [2]. Check that bubble [4] is in exact center of scale.

If bubble [4] is in exact center of scale, strip [2] is vertical. Go to Step 9.

If bubble [4] is not in exact center of scale, strip [2] is not vertical. Continue.

Shims [1] are placed behind strip [2] to make strip vertical. Shims of different thicknesses may be needed.

When adjusting strip [2], hold carpenter's level against facing edge of strip. Insert small shim behind strip. Move shim up and down strip until bubble [4] is in exact center of scale.

7. Insert shim [1] behind strip [2]. Move shim until bubble [4] is in exact center of scale. Secure shim by driving nail through strip and into wall.

8. Install as many shims as needed to plumb and support strip [2]. Secure each shim by driving nail through strip, shim, and into wall.

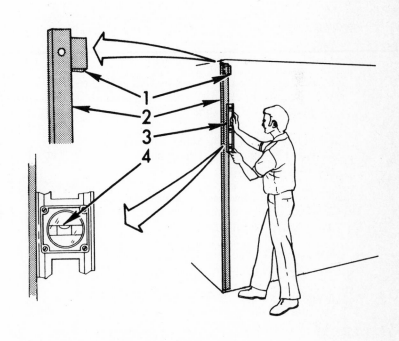

Nails are placed at 12-inch intervals.

9. Nail strip [2] to wall.

10. Repeat Step 2 through Step 9 to install and plumb remaining strips.

17

PREPARATION FOR PANELING

▶ Framing a Wall

Before framing a wall, be sure to consider the following:

- A frame [1] will extend the wall surface several inches into room.

- Door frames and window frames will have to be changed accordingly to make them flush with new wall surface.

- Electrical outlets, switches, and fixtures, as well as any plumbing and heating facilities, will have to be moved or changed to fit new wall surface.

A frame [1] can be constructed from 2 in. x 3 in. or 2 in. x 4 in. studs. The 2 in. x 4 in. studs can be positioned sideways [2] so that less room space is lost to framing.

Fasteners needed to attach a frame to a ceiling and floor depend upon type of ceiling and floor material.

For example, in attaching a frame to a concrete floor, masonry tools and fasteners are needed.

Concrete block or masonry walls must be waterproofed before a frame [1] is installed. Seal the wall with cement sealer. A paint dealer will help you select a good sealer.

Framing a wall is often the best way of preparing a wall for paneling. For example, if you live in a rented house or apartment where it may be necessary to remove the paneling at a later time, you should consider constructing a frame and then paneling the frame. There need be little or no damage to the wall.

If you wish to panel a concrete block or masonry wall, framing the wall is preferrable to installing furring strips. Framing results in minimum damage to the wall. In addition, if the wall is subject to dampness, such as in a basement, you should consider using a frame because it can be constructed to permit good ventilation between the wall and the paneling.

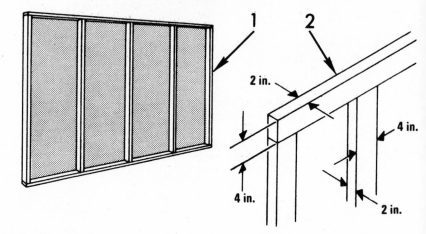

Framing a Wall

1. Measure and record width of wall.

2. Measure and cut two 2 in. x 4 in. studs [2, 3] to width recorded in Step 1. They will become the plate [2] and the shoe [3] of the frame.

3. Measure height of wall. Subtract thickness of plate [2] and shoe [3] from height and record measurement.

If wall or floor will be subject to dampness, subtract 1/4-inch from measurement to allow for gap between shoe [3] and floor.

4. Mark plate [2] and shoe [3] at 16-inch intervals to indicate centers of studs [4].

5. Determine number of studs [4] needed. Measure and cut studs to length determined in Step 3.

6. Construct frame by nailing studs [4] at 16-inch intervals to plate [2] and shoe [3].

If wall will be subject to dampness, go to Step 7.

If wall will not be subject to dampness, go to Step 9.

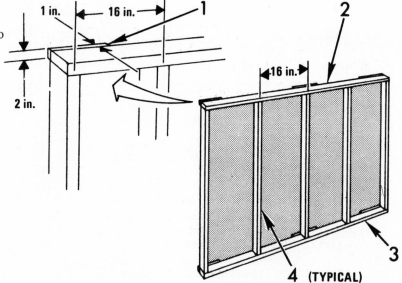

7. Measure and cut six 1-foot blocks [1] from 1 in. x 2 in. lengths of wood.

8. Attach blocks [1] to frame at four corners and at center of plate [2] and shoe [3].

18

Framing a Wall

9. Place frame at installed position against wall.

Frame is plumb if it makes 90° angle with floor. Carpenter's level is used to check if frame is plumb.

10. Place carpenter's level against facing edge of middle stud [3]. Check that bubble [1] is in exact center of scale.

If bubble [1] is in exact center of scale, frame is plumb. Go to Step 14.

If bubble [1] is not in exact center of scale, continue.

Shims [2] are placed between plate [4] or shoe [5] and wall to make frame plumb.

When adjusting frame, check plumb by holding carpenter's level against facing edge of middle stud [3].

11. Place shims [2] between frame and wall until bubble is in exact center of scale.

12. Remove frame from wall. Nail shims to shoe or plate.

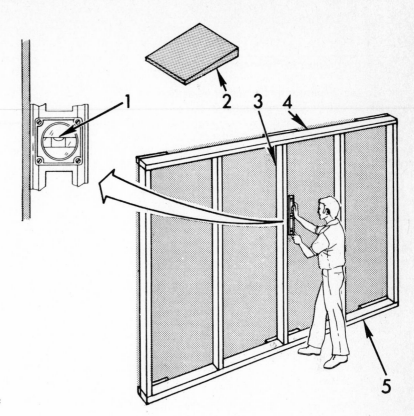

Framing a Wall

13. Place frame at installed position.

14. While holding frame at installed position, drive wedges [2] under bottom of frame to hold frame tightly against ceiling.

15. Attach frame to ceiling.

16. Remove wedges [2], if not required for providing gap between shoe [1] and floor.

17. Attach frame to floor.

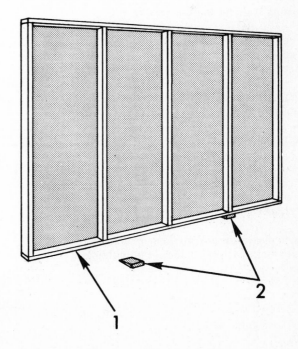

▶ **Cutting Veneered Plywood Sheet Panels**

To avoid splintering the veneer while cutting, observe the following practices:

When cutting a panel by hand, use a crosscut saw with 10 or more teeth to the inch. Never use a rip saw for cutting plywood. Veneer or other surfaces will splinter badly.

When cutting a panel with a circular saw, use a hollow-ground combination blade.

Depending on the type of saw being used, the panel must be turned with the veneer facing either up or down:

Crosscut Saw	Face Veneer Up
Table Saw	Face Veneer Up
Radial Arm Saw	Face Veneer Down
Portable Circular Saw	Face Veneer Down
Sabre Saw	Face Veneer Down

When cutting a sheet panel, be sure to support both sections evenly to prevent panel from splintering.

If, after you observe the above rules, the veneer still splinters, you might try applying masking tape over the line to be cut. However, you must be careful on removing the tape after sawing the cut, or the tape itself will pull splinters from the veneer.

Another procedure to reduce splintering is to first score the line to be cut with a sharp knife. Then saw it.

▶ **Cutting Molding and Baseboards**

A coped joint is used when molding is fitted at an inside corner [1]. Go to Page 21 for cutting a coped joint.

A miter joint is used when molding is fitted at an outside corner [2].

▶ **Cutting a Miter Joint**

A miter joint is cut so that two pieces of molding are joined together to make a 90° angle.

Each piece of molding is cut at a 45° angle.

When measuring and marking molding, be sure to place mark [3] on inside edge of molding.

1. Measure and mark [3] molding.

2. Place molding in miter box. Using mark [3] as a guide, cut molding.

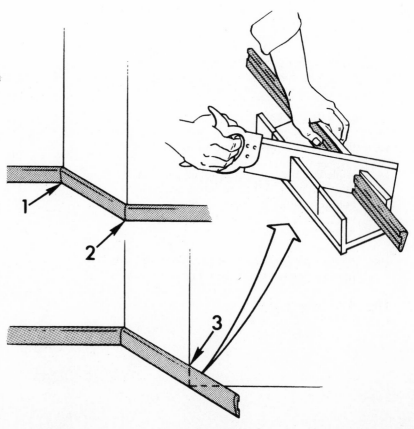

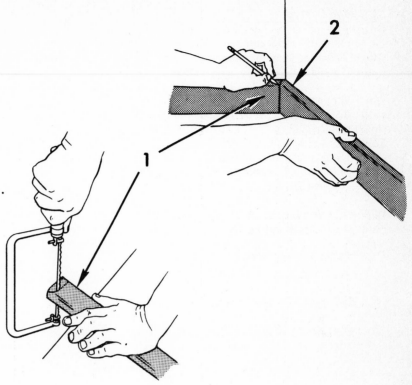

▶ Cutting a Coped Joint

1. Place and hold molding [1] at installed position. Place another piece of molding [2] against molding [1].

2. Draw outline of molding [2] on molding [1].

3. Using coping saw, cut molding [1] along outline.

4. Using sandpaper, lightly sand cut.

▶ Locating Cutouts

Instructions in this section tell how to locate and make cutouts for electrical switches and outlets.

If you are installing soft panels or boards, you may be able to mark cutouts by holding board or panel against switch or outlet junction box and tapping it with a board and hammer to leave an impression of the opening. If this is not possible, the location of cutouts must be determined by measurement.

Electrical switch and outlet cover plates must be removed.

1. Measure and record distances [1, 2] from edges of opening to edge of panel.

When measuring distances [3, 4] from floor to screws, be sure to subtract any distance [5] the panel will be above floor when panel is installed.

2. Measure and record distances [3, 4] from floor to screws. Subtract distance [5].

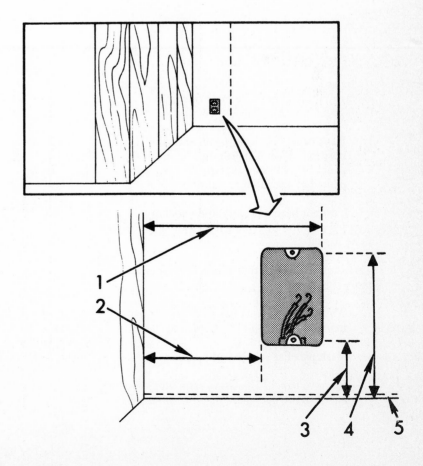

MEASURING AND CUTTING

Locating Cutouts

When making marks and lines on paneling, make them lightly so they may be easily removed when cutout is made.

3. On panel to be cut, measure and mark distances [1, 2, 4, 5] recorded in Step 1 and 2.

4. Using a carpenter's square, make four straight lines through marks to indicate location of cutout [3].

Center of drill bit should be placed inside marked area at corners of cutout [3].

5. Using drill and 3/8-inch bit, make hole [6] at four corners of marked area.

6. Using keyhole saw, carefully cut opening.

7. Using medium grit sandpaper, smooth cut edges.

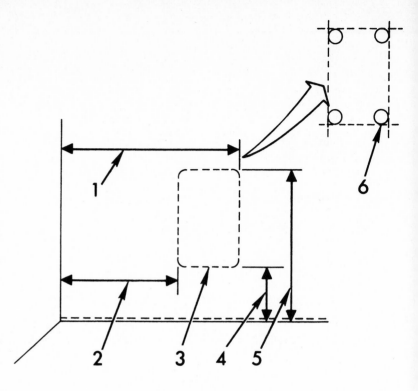

▶ **Cutting Around Doors**

If you are not planning to butt paneling against existing molding, molding must be removed. Door and hinges may have to be removed.

1. Place panel [2] against wall at installed position. Push it tightly against installed panel [4]. Be sure that gap [5] between panel [2] and floor is maintained.

If you do not have a helper, hold panel in installed position by nailing it to wall in two places along top edge.

Mark panel lightly so that marks can be removed easily if required.

2. While holding panel [2] at installed position, mark panel at top [1] of opening.

3. Mark panel at side [3] of opening.

4. Remove panel [2]. Using carpenter's square and straightedge, mark opening on panel.

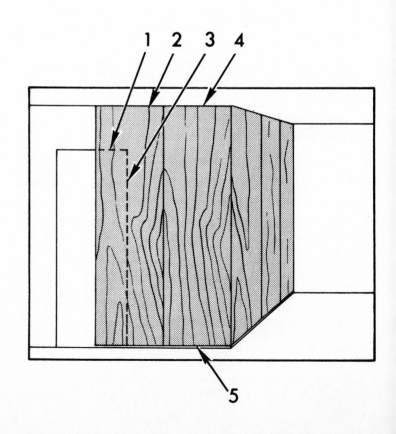

Cutting Around Doors

Size of cutout depends upon how door molding is planned to be used.

If door is to be concealed (no molding used), cutout [1] must be same size as opening.

If cap molding [4] will be used around door, increase size of opening by distance [3] to allow for overlap between cap [4] and door frame [2]. Be sure to make cutout large enough to allow for uneven frame [2].

If casing molding [8] with rabbet [6] will be used around door, increase size of opening by distance [7]. Be sure that casing molding [8] will overlap paneling [5].

If other types of molding are used, determine correct size of cutout.

5. Using marking of opening on panel as a guide, increase size of cutout as required.

6. Mark size of cutout on panel.

7. Cut panel. Sand rough edges with sandpaper.

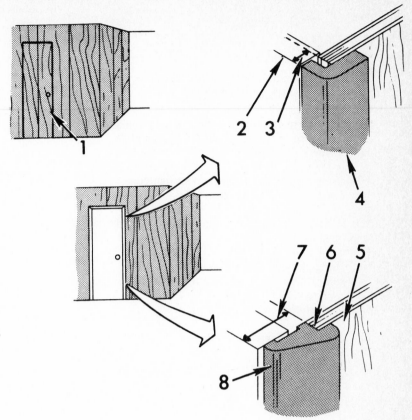

▶**Cutting Around Windows**

If you are not planning to butt paneling against existing molding, molding must be removed.

1. Place panel [2] against wall at installed position. Push it tightly against installed panel [1]. Be sure that gap [5] between panel [2] and floor is maintained.

2. While holding panel [2] at installed position, place marks [4] on edge of panel to indicate top and bottom of window opening.

3. Measure and record distance [3] from top mark to edge of window. Measure and record distance [6] from bottom mark to edge of window.

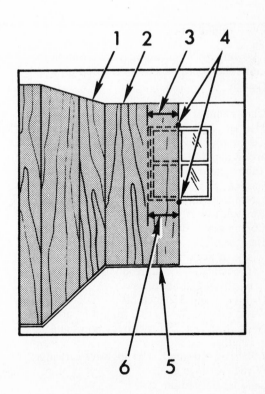

Cutting Around Windows

When making marks and lines on paneling, make them lightly so they can be easily removed after cut is made.

4. Using carpenter's square and straightedge, mark opening [1] on panel.

Size of cutout depends upon how window molding is planned to be used.

5. Using marking of opening on panel as a guide, increase size of cutout as required.

6. Mark size of cutout on panel.

7. Cut panel. Sand rough edges.

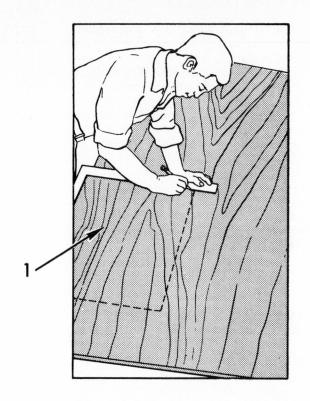

■ INSTALLING PANELS ■

▶ **Tools and Supplies**

The following tools and supplies are required for installing solid board panels or veneered plywood sheet panels:

> Claw hammer [1]
> Nail set [2]
> Common screwdriver [3]
> Wood rasp [4]
> Tape measure [5]
> Carpenter's square [6]
> Carpenter's level [7]
> Keyhole saw [8] or sabre saw [9]
> Coping saw [10]
> Hand saw [11] or table saw or radial arm saw or portable circular saw or sabre saw. If cutting plywood, read Page 20 for selection and use of saw.
> Drill [12] and 3/8-inch bit
> Wood blocks. Pieces of 2 in. x 4 in. are best.
> Nails. See Page 28 for correct types and lengths.
> Adhesive, if desired. Use adhesive cartridges and cartridge gun.
> Sandpaper, medium grit

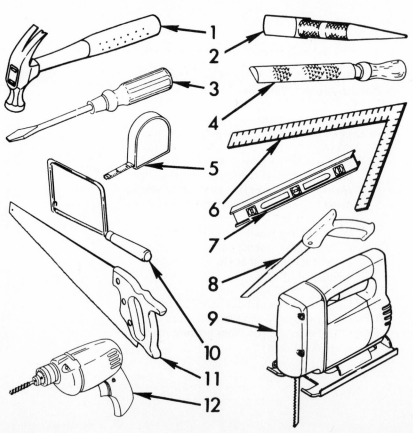

▶ **Installing Solid Board Panels Vertically**

Before beginning to install panels, determine use of molding and trim at ceiling, floors, inside corners, outside corners, windows, doors, and obstacles.

Solid board panels may be installed with nails or adhesive. Finishing nails are recommended. Nails should be long enough to extend 3/4-inch into furring.

Cutouts for electrical switches and outlets, doors and windows, must be made before each panel is installed.

Horizontal furring strips must be installed. If installing paneling in basement where dampness is a problem, leave 1/4-inch gap at top and bottom of panel. Gaps will allow circulation of air. Special ceiling molding with slits is available to cover gap at ceiling and allow air to circulate.

In other areas, if molding is to be installed along ceiling, leave 1/4-inch gap [1] between top of panel [2] and ceiling. If not installing molding, place panel against ceiling.

Begin installing panels at a corner and work across the wall.

1. Place panel [2] against wall. Push panel tightly into corner.

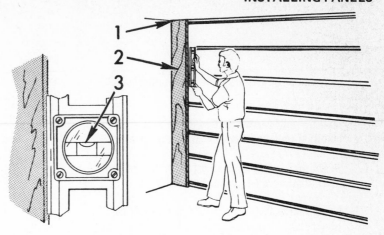

First panel installed must be plumb. Panel is plumb if bubble [3] is in exact center of scale.

2. Place carpenter's level against edge of panel [2]. Check that bubble [3] is in exact center of scale.

If bubble [3] is not in exact center of scale, panel [2] is not plumb. Panel must be cut to fit corner before continuing. While holding panel plumb, mark panel with cutout of corner. Cut panel to fit corner.

If panel is plumb, continue.

Installing Solid Board Panels Vertically

If width of panel [4] is 6 inches or less, two nails [2] are used at each end of panel and at each furring strip [3].

If width of panel [4] is more than 6 inches, three nails [1] are used at each end of panel and at each furring strip [3].

3. Place first panel [4] at installed position. Nail panel to wall. Use nailset to sink head of nail below surface of panel.

If installing tongue and groove panels [5], remaining panels use one nail [7] at each end of panel and at each furring strip [3]. Nails are driven through tongue [6] at 50° angle [8].

For panels other than tongue and groove panels, use same nail pattern as first panel [4].

4. Working one panel at a time, install remaining panels except last panel.

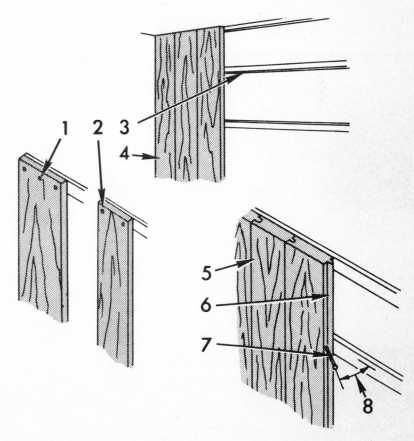

Installing Solid Board Panels Vertically

Last panel must be fitted between installed panel and wall.

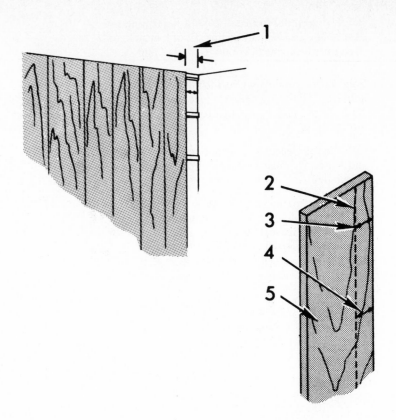

5.   Measure and record distance [1] between installed panel and corner at several places.

6.   Beginning at edge of panel [5], measure and mark distances [4] recorded in Step 5.

7.   Using marks [3] as guide, draw line [2] on panel [5].

8.   Using line [2] as a guide, cut panel [5].

If panel [5] does not fit between installed panel and corner, file it until it fits.

Nail pattern used to install last panel [5] is same as nail pattern used for first panel.

9.   Place last panel [5] at installed position. Nail panel to wall.

▶ **Installing Solid Board Panels Horizontally**

Before beginning paneling, determine use of molding and trim at ceiling, floors, inside corners, outside corners, windows, doors and obstacles.

Solid board panels may be installed with nails or adhesive. Finishing nails are recommended. Nails should be long enough to extend 3/4-inch into furring strips or studs.

Cutouts for electrical switches and outlets, doors and windows, must be made before each panel is installed.

Begin installing panels at the floor and work toward the ceiling.

If tongue and groove or shiplap joint panels are used, position panel so that tongue [3] is faced up.

If paneling basement where dampness is a problem, leave 1/4-inch gap between first panel and floor and between last panel and ceiling. Gaps will allow circulation of air. Special ceiling molding with slits is available to cover gap at ceiling and allow air to circulate.

In other areas, if floor molding is to be used, allow 1/4-inch gap between panel and floor.

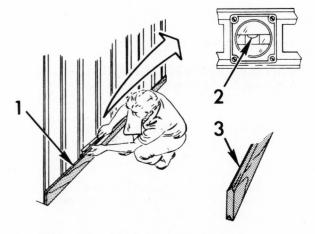

1.   Place panel [1] against wall and floor.

First panel installed must be level. Panel is level if bubble [2] is in exact center of scale.

2.   Place carpenter's level on top edge of panel [1]. Check that bubble [2] is in exact center of scale.

If bubble [2] is not in exact center of scale, panel [1] is not level. Panel must be scribed before continuing.

If panel is level, continue.

Installing Solid Board Panels Horizontally

If width of panel [3] is 6 inches or less, two nails [2] are used at each end of panel and at each furring strip or stud [1].

3. Place first panel [4] at installed position. Install panel by driving required nails through panel.

If installing tongue and groove panels [5], remaining panels use one nail [6] at each end of panel and at each furring strip or stud [1]. Nails are driven through tongue [7] at 50° angle.

Panels other than tongue and groove panels use same nail pattern as first panel [4].

4. Working one panel at a time, install remaining panels except last panel.

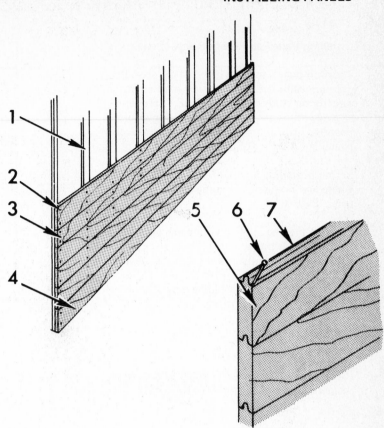

Installing Solid Board Panels Horizontally

If ceiling molding will be used, allow 1/4-inch gap between last panel and ceiling.

If no molding will be used, last panel must be fitted between installed panel [1] and ceiling [2].

5. Measure and record distance between installed panel [1] and ceiling at several places. Subtract 1/4-inch from longest distance if gap is required.

6. Measure and mark panel [3] with distance(s) recorded in Step 5.

7. Using mark(s) as guide, draw line on panel [3].

8. Cut panel [3].

If panel does not fit between installed panel [1] and ceiling, trim it until it fits.

Nail pattern used to install last panel [3] is same as used for first panel.

9. Place last panel [3] at installed position. Nail panel to wall.

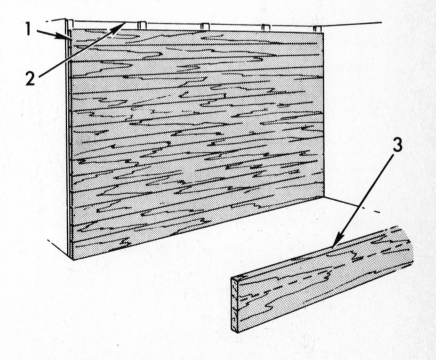

INSTALLING PANELS

▶ Installing Veneered Plywood Sheet Panels

Plywood panels may be installed on plaster or gypsum wallboard walls or they may be installed directly on studs or furring strips. Frequently, exposed studs are first covered with gypsum board to provide a firmer, smoother surface for paneling. A better quality paneling job will result.

Before beginning any paneling, first determine where and how you are going to use molding and trim. Page 3.

Paneling may be applied with panel adhesive or nails. The advantage of using adhesives is that the panel surface is unmarked by depressions that result from the use of nails. Adhesives give a better appearing job. Molding may also be applied with panel adhesive.

If using panel adhesive to install panels, go to Page 30.

If using nails to install panels, go to next section (below). Select nails from chart.

Surface	Nails
Furring strips, studs, backing board	3 penny (1-1/4 in.) finishing nails or 1 in. colored nails
Gypsum wallboard, plaster walls	6 penny (2 in.) finishing nails or 1-5/8 in. colored nails
Molding and trim	3 penny (1-1/4 in.) finishing nails or 1-5/8 in. colored nails

1. Finishing nails must be countersunk 1/32 inch. Use nailset to countersink nails to avoid damage to surfaces. Colored putty which blends with panel finishes is available for filling countersunk holes.

2. Colored nails are not countersunk. Colors are available to blend with many panel colors.

▶ Installing Veneered Plywood Sheet Panels with Nails — First Panel on a Wall

Cutouts for electrical switches and outlets, doors and windows must be made before panel is installed.

If molding is to be installed along ceiling, leave 1/4-inch gap [1] between top of panel [2] and ceiling. If not installing molding, place panel against ceiling.

Panel [2] must be located so that edge [3] is on center of stud [4] or furring strip. First panel on a wall must be plumb. Therefore, center of stud [4] must be marked with a plumb line, Page 13.

Edge [5] of panel [2] must fit corner.

1. Trim panel [2] so that edge [5] fits corner and edge [4] is aligned with plumb line.

2. Drive four nails [6] part way into panel [2] 1 inch from top edge.

3. Place panel [2] at installed position.

4. While holding panel at installed position, drive four nails [6] into wall.

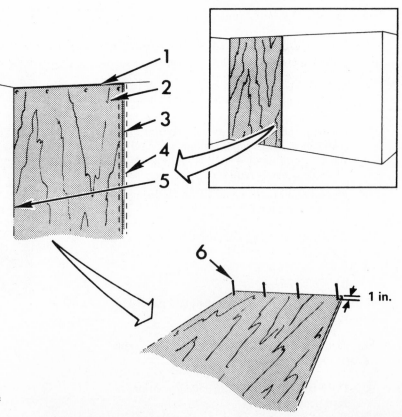

28

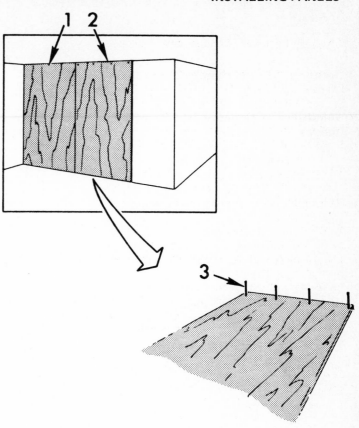

▶ Installing Veneered Plywood Sheet Panels with Nails — Middle Panels

Cutouts for electrical switches, outlets, doors and windows must be made before panels are installed.

1. Drive four nails [3] through top edge of panel [2] until ends of nails just show.

2. Place panel [2] against wall. Push panel against installed panel [1].

3. Drive four nails [3] completely into wall.

4. Repeat Step 1 through Step 3 for each panel except last panel on wall.

Go to next section (below) for installation of last panel on wall.

▶ Installing Veneered Plywood Sheet Panels with Nails — Last Panel on a Wall

Cutouts for electrical switches, outlets, doors and windows must be made before panel is installed.

1. Measure and record distance [2] between installed panel [1] and corner at several places.

2. Beginning at edge of panel [3], measure and mark distances [2] recorded in Step 1.

3. Using marks as guides, draw line on panel [3].

4. Cut panel. Sand rough edges with sandpaper.

If panel does not fit, trim it until it fits.

5. Drive two nails through top edge of panel [3] until ends of nails just show.

6. Place panel [3] at installed position. Push panel tightly against installed panel [1].

7. Drive nails into wall.

Go to Page 30 for completing nailing of panels to walls.

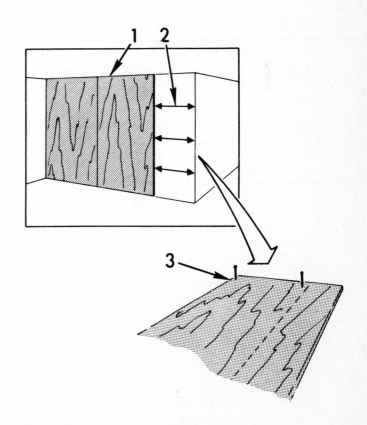

▶ **Installing Veneered Plywood Sheet Panels with Nails — All Panels**

If installing panels onto studs [2], space nails as follows:

    4-inch intervals [1] at four edges
    12-inch intervals [3] at each stud [2]

If installing sheet panels onto furring strips [4], space nails as follows:

    4-inch intervals [1] at four edges
    16-inch intervals [4] at each horizontal furring strip [5]

If installing sheet panels directly onto wall, be sure that nails hit studs. Space nails as follows:

    4-inch intervals [1] at four edges
    16-inch intervals [6] at each wall stud [7]

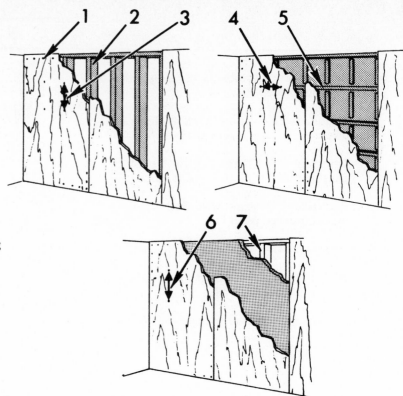

▶ **Installing Veneered Plywood Sheet Panels with Adhesive — First Panel on a Wall**

Cutouts for electrical switches and outlets, doors and windows must be made before panel is installed.

If molding is to be installed along ceiling, leave 1/4-inch gap [1] between top of panel [2] and ceiling. If not installing molding, place panel against ceiling.

If panels are fastened to wall with panel adhesive, the edges of the panel will sometimes separate from the wall. Separation can occur as a result of improper application of panel adhesive. So that edges of panels can be attached to wall with nails if adhesive fails at a later time, it is a good idea for edges [3] to be located on centers of studs [4] or furring strips.

First panel on a wall must be plumb. Therefore wall must be marked with a plumb line for aligning edge [3] of panel. Go to Page 13 for marking a plumb line.

Edge [5] of panel [2] must fit corner.

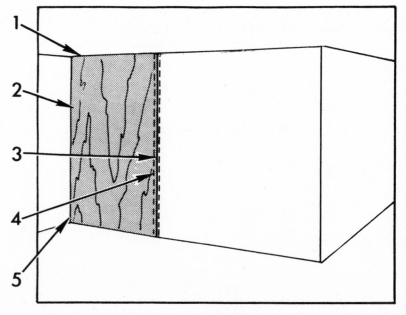

Installing Veneered Plywood Sheet Panels with
Adhesive – First Panel on a Wall

1. Trim panel [3] so that edge [1] fits corner
    and edge [2] is aligned with plumb line.

2. Drive four 3 penny (1-1/4 inch) finishing
    nails [4] partway into panel [3] 1 inch
    from top edge.

3. Following manufacturer's instructions, apply
    panel adhesive to wall, studs or furring strips.
    Do not apply adhesive beyond area to be
    covered by panel.

4. Place panel [3] at installed position.

5. While holding panel at installed position,
    drive four nails [4] 1/4-inch to 1/2-inch into
    wall. Be sure that nail heads extend from
    panel enough for easy removal of nails.

6. Press entire surface of panel [3] against wall
    to spread adhesive.

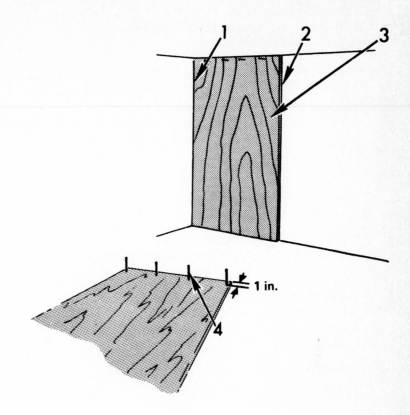

Installing Veneered Plywood Sheet Panels with
Adhesive – First Panel on a Wall

7. Carefully pull bottom edge of panel [1] 8 or
    10 inches from wall to allow air to get to
    adhesive. Place block between panel and wall
    to hold panel from wall.

Panel must be held from wall for 8 to 10 minutes
or as long as adhesive manufacturer recommends
to allow adhesive to become tacky.

8. Remove block. Press panel [1] against wall.

9. Using hammer and block of wood padded
    with cloth, tap panel [1] against wall at edges
    and over entire surface.

10. Wipe off excess adhesive.

11. Remove nails or, using nailset, countersink
    nails and fill holes with colored putty.

Go to Page 32 for installation of remaining panels
on wall.

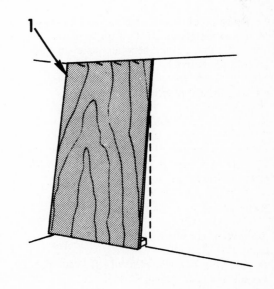

INSTALLING PANELS

▶ **Installing Veneered Plywood Sheet Panels with Adhesive — Middle Panels**

Cutouts for electrical switches and outlets, doors and windows must be made before panels are installed.

1. Drive four 3 penny finishing nails [3] partway into panel [2] 1 inch from top edge.

2. Following manufacturer's instructions, apply panel adhesive to wall, studs or furring strips. Do not apply adhesive beyond area covered by panel.

3. Place panel [2] at installed position. Be sure that edge [1] is against edge of panel previously installed.

4. While holding panel at installed position, drive four nails [3] 1/4-inch to 1/2-inch into wall. Be sure that nail heads extend from panel enough for easy removal of nails.

5. Press entire surface of panel [2] against wall to spread adhesive.

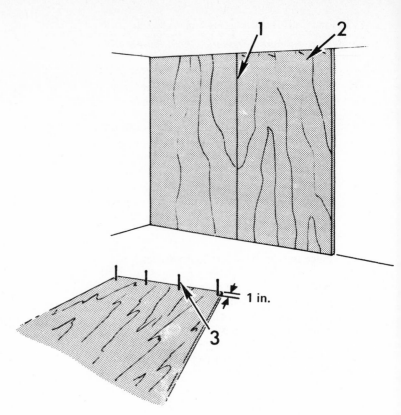

Installing Veneered Plywood Sheet Panels with Adhesive — Middle Panels

6. Carefully pull bottom edge of panel [1] 8 or 10 inches from wall to allow air to get to adhesive. Place block between panel and wall to hold panel from wall.

7. Allow adhesive to become tacky.

8. Remove block. Press panel [1] against wall.

9. Using hammer and block of wood padded with cloth, tap panel [1] against wall at edges and over entire surface.

10. Wipe off excess adhesive.

11. Remove or countersink nails.

12. Repeat Step 1 through Step 11 for each panel except last panel on wall.

Go to Page 33 for installation of last panel on wall.

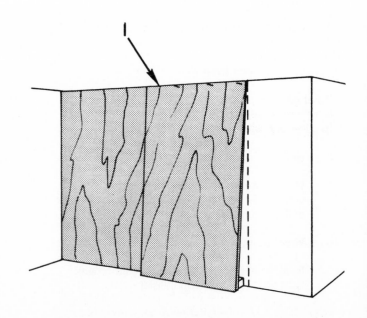

▶ **Installing Veneered Plywood Sheet Panels with Adhesive — Last Panel**

Cutouts for electrical switches and outlets, doors and windows must be made before panels are installed.

1. Measure and record distance [2] between installed panel [1] and corner at several places.

2. Beginning at edge [4] of panel [3], measure and mark distances recorded in Step 1.

3. Using marks as guides, draw line on panel [3].

4. Cut panel [3]. Sand rough edges with sandpaper.

If panel does not fit, trim it until it fits.

5. Drive two 3 penny nails part way into panel [3] 1 inch from top edge.

6. Go to Page 32 and perform Step 2 through Step 11.

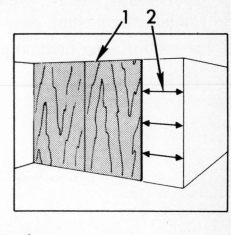

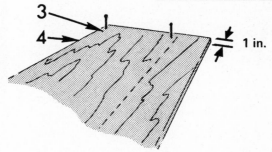

1 in.

One of the most popular uses for paneling is one to which it is ideally suited: the casual, easy-care decor of a comfortable, inviting playroom or den.

The conveniently located family room is paneled with the same Weldwood ''Vinylgard'' that covers the kitchen wall a few steps away. *Photo courtesy of Champion Building Products, Champion International Corp., Stamford, Conn.* (right)

This artist's cozy hideway features ''Old World'' cedar paneling from Georgia-Pacific. *Photo courtesy of Georgia-Pacific Corporation.* (below)

The nautical motif of this den alcove draws its rustic charm from a brick floor, hooked rug, and Weldwood ''Oak Grove,'' a woodgrain print that reproduces the texture of natural oak hardwood. *Photo courtesy of Champion Building Products, Champion International Corp., Stamford, Conn.* (below right)

Paneling is well suited to more formal uses, too, as these living rooms convincingly illustrate.

The combination of vertical and horizontal ''Knotty Birch'' panels adds warmth to the charm of this booklover's retreat. *Photo courtesy of Georgia-Pacific Corporation.* (above left)

The indoor garden in this sunny living room is framed by Weldwood Craftsman II ''Charter Pecan'' paneling. *Photo courtesy of Champion Building Products, Champion International Corp., Stamford, Conn.* (above right)

Simplicity is opulent when antique furnishings and wood parquet floor are set off by a backdrop of ''Barnstable,'' a simulated barn plank embossed on hardboard. *Photo courtesy of Masonite Corporation.* (left)

Bedrooms take on a striking new dimension with wood paneling.

Pastel-toned paneling converts unfinished attic space to a sleep, storage, and study area for a young male occupant. The wood wall covering is Weldwood "Candyland," priced to meet tight budgets and designed to add a dash of color to any room in the house. *Photo courtesy of Champion Building Products, Champion International Corp., Stamford, Conn.* (right)

Wicker accents and straw matting harmonize with "Cedarglen River-rock" paneling to give this bedroom the snug homeyness of a country cabin. *Photo courtesy of Georgia-Pacific Corporation.* (below)

Nothing is quite so effective as paneling in pulling together separate-but-adjoining living spaces.

In this classic vacation-home interior, rustic "Barnplank" paneling fills the downstairs living area and continues upstairs to the sleeping quarters. The same paneling is shown in another hearthside setting on the back cover of this book. *Photo courtesy of Georgia-Pacific Corporation.* (top)

The more contemporary, streamlined look of this all-purpose living space is brightened by skylights and "Ol' Savannah — Carpenter's Pine" installed in vertical and horizontal panels. "Ol' Savannah — Chandler's Pine" decorates the country bedroom on the back cover. *Photo courtesy of Georgia-Pacific Corporation.* (above)

"Mural Pecan" paneling is an elegant but unobtrusive backdrop to the dining area of a larger room. *Photo courtesy of Georgia-Pacific Corporation.* (bottom left)

DECORATIVE WALL COVERINGS

Many types of decorative wall coverings are available for today's homeowner. Some of the most popular wall coverings are cork, mirror, and simulated brick.

These wall coverings can be installed with professional results by almost anyone willing to plan carefully and work slowly. They are not difficult to install.

The selection of the type of wall covering to install is largely a matter of personal preference. Books about interior decorating are full of ideas regarding the use of different wall coverings.

The following paragraphs describe cork, mirror, and simulated brick wall coverings. Before selecting and installing a wall covering, be sure to read these paragraphs.

▶ **Cork Tiles**

Cork tiles are available in a variety of textures and tones, including natural and colored finishes.

Cork tile has many properties which make it an ideal wall covering:

- Cork resists scratches and dents because of its natural construction, making it very functional in areas of activity (playroom, family room).

- Cork is a natural insulation — it helps keep rooms warmer in the winter and cooler in the summer. Noise insulation is also provided.

- Light vacuuming or wiping with a damp cloth is the only care needed.

- Many brands of cork tile are fire-resistant.

Cork Tiles

Cork tiles are commonly available in the following sizes:

　　6 in. x 12 in.
　　12 in. x 12 in.
　　12 in. x 24 in.
　　24 in. x 48 in.

Thicknesses range from 1/8- to 3/4-inches.

Cork tiles must be stored in the room to be tiled for at least 24 hours before installation. Because cork is a natural wood material, it must be allowed to expand or contract according to room temperature.

Many manufacturers recommend installing cork tiles with a cork tile adhesive. This is especially true if covering entire walls or large areas with cork.

An alternate method of installation is the use of double-face tape. This method is quick, and should be considered for small tiling applications.

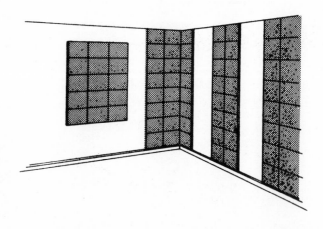

Regardless of the method used, be careful when handling cork tiles. Some grades of cork are extremely fragile and can crumble or break easily.

To finish off your tiled area and to protect cork edges, molding is sometimes installed. Go to Page 2 for a description of the styles and applications of wood molding.

▶ Mirror Tiles

Mirror tiles are available in a wide variety of styles and patterns. Designs vary, including antique, geometric, abstract, prints, and wood grain — almost any design to fit your decorative talents.

Mirror tiles are an excellent way to effectively enlarge any room, hallway or entryway. Because cleaning is so easy, mirror is often used as a functional wall covering in kitchens and bathrooms, while still producing a decorative touch.

In addition to mirror tiles with individual styles and patterns, mirror murals can be purchased which depict innumerable subjects and designs. Murals are an attractive decorative item which can enhance any room. Murals are commonly composed of six or more mirror tiles.

Nearly all mirror tiles, including tiles for murals, are commonly available in sizes of 12 in. x 12 in.

Double-face tape is used to install mirror tiles. Tile manufacturers sometime include tape in each mirror tile package. Some tiles have the tape already applied to the back of each tile.

Be careful when handling mirror tiles. As with any other glass product, breakage is easy and can result in personal injury.

To finish off your tiled area and to protect mirror edges, decorative molding is sometimes installed. Go to Page 2 for a description of the styles and applications of wood molding.

▶ Simulated Bricks

Simulated bricks are available in a variety of realistic styles, textures and colors, ranging from standard brick (red, gold, white) to rustic and used brick.

Simulated bricks give a warm decorative touch to any living area. Bricks are easily cleaned and very resistant to damage, making them an excellent wall covering for active areas of your home.

The most popular types of simulated bricks are lightweight and fire-resistant. Most will not melt or discolor when exposed to heat, such as near a fireplace or cooking area.

Simulated bricks are normally 1/4 in. to 3/8 in. thick. Lengths and widths are standard brick sizes.

Adhesive is used to install simulated bricks. The adhesive is spread onto the wall, and the bricks are then laid into it. The adhesive dries to a realistic mortar finish.

A clear sealer is sometimes applied over the finished brick wall. The sealer forms a protective coating for easy cleaning.

Wall surfaces on which decorative wall coverings are installed must be sound and in good condition.

Surfaces must be flat and level with no high or low spots. This is especially true if installing mirror tiles. Mirror tiles accentuate any irregularities across the surface.

Adhesives used to install decorative wall coverings require a smooth, clean surface. Check that painted surfaces are not chipped or peeling. Wallpapered surfaces must have the old wallpaper removed.

If there is dirt, grease, or wax, it must be removed. Following manufacturer's instructions, mix a solution of trisodium phosphate (T.S.P.). Wash surface with solution.

■■ CORK TILES ■■

▶ **Planning and Estimating**

Planning for installation of cork tiles depends entirely on your own decorative abilities and preferences. The variety of uses for cork tile is almost endless.

You may decide to cover all walls in a room or just a single wall, or make cork strips spaced at intervals of your own choosing. Maybe an attractive bulletin board or pin-up space is desired.

Regardless of how you decide to use cork tiles, estimate the amount of tiles and adhesive by performing the following steps:

1. Make a scale drawing of the surfaces to be covered. Include any fixtures and obstacles (doors, windows) not to be covered.

2. Take the drawing to the dealer. He will tell you the number of tiles and amount of adhesive or double-face tape required.

▶ **Tools and Supplies**

The following tools and supplies are required to install cork tiles:

- A flexible metal rule [1] to measure areas to be tiled

- A straightedge [2] to aid in cutting tiles in straight lines. A metal edge is recommended, but any straight object can be used.

- A sharp knife [3] to cut tiles

- A carpenter's square [4] to mark a 90° angle for first tile installed

- A plumb [5] to give a true, straight vertical line as a guide for installing tiles. A plumb can be constructed of a piece of string, some colored chalk, and any object suitable for a weight.

- A notched trowel [6] to install adhesive, or scissors [7] to cut double-face tape

- Drop cloths to protect floor surface if using adhesive to install tiles

▶ **Marking the Wall**

Having decided the application and pattern of your tile installation, you must mark a 90° angle on the wall as a guide for installing tiles. This ensures that all tiles are installed squarely on the wall.

Wall surfaces must be prepared before marking the wall. Page 42.

A 90° angle is made with a plumb line [3] and chalk line [1].

Read the following paragraphs to determine where to mark the 90° angle for your specific application.

If installing tiles in a small area [2], such as for a bulletin board or pin-up space, make the 90° angle at one corner of the area. Go to Page 44, Step 1 to mark the wall.

If installing tiles on an entire wall [5], or in vertical rows [4] which reach the ceiling, several considerations must be made to determine where to make the 90° angle. Go to Page 44 (top).

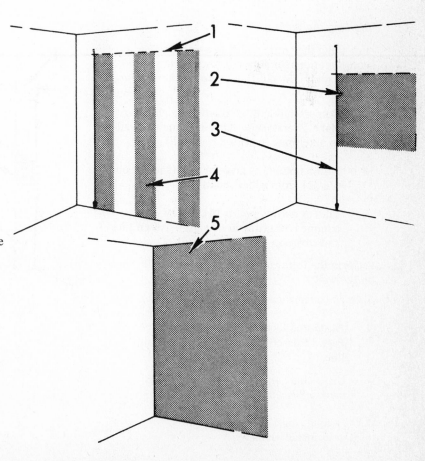

CORK TILES

Marking the Wall

For single vertical rows of tiles [2], no 90° angle is needed. A plumb line [1] is made at the edge of each row. Go to Step 2 to mark the plumb line.

For adjacent vertical rows of tiles [7], consider the following:

● The ceiling may not be exactly straight. Make several measurements from floor to ceiling to determine the highest point [3] along the ceiling.

● Chalk line [6] is made at a distance of one tile [4] from the highest point [3].

● Tiles at low points [5] can be easily trimmed, resulting in no gaps between tiles and ceiling.

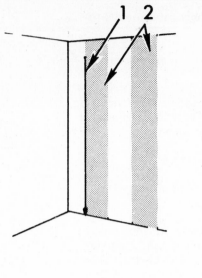

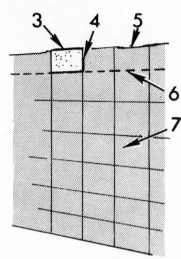

Marking the Wall

For tiling the entire width of a wall, the considerations for adjacent rows of tiles above apply. In addition, consider the following:

● Corners may not be exactly straight. Make several measurements along the wall to determine its widest point [1].

● Plumb line [3] is made at a distance of one tile [2] from widest point [1].

● Tiles at narrow points [4] can be easily trimmed, resulting in no gaps between tiles and corners.

Perform the following steps to mark the 90° angle on the wall:

1. Determine location of 90° angle.

2. At desired location, mark a plumb line [7]. Page 13 describes how to mark a plumb line.

3. Using chalk and carpenter's square [6], mark a 90° angle to plumb line [7].

4. Extend chalk line [5] as required for your installation.

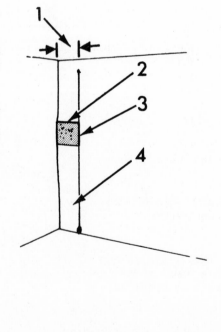

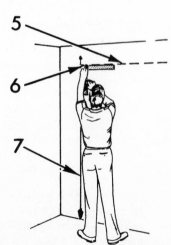

▶ **Cutting Tiles**

Cork tiles may require cutting to fit around fixtures [1], or around ceiling and wall borders [2] or obstacles such as doors and windows.

For fixtures [1], remove the fixture cover. Measure and mark the tile [5] to match the wall opening.

For ceiling and wall borders [2], and for obstacles, measure and mark the tile [4] according to the space to be covered.

Perform the following steps to cut the tile:

1. Align straightedge with marks [3] if required.

Tile must be cut with a sharp knife. Use a back and forth motion, making small cuts at a time. Cut gently to prevent crumbling tile edges.

2. Using sharp knife or razor blade, cut tile.

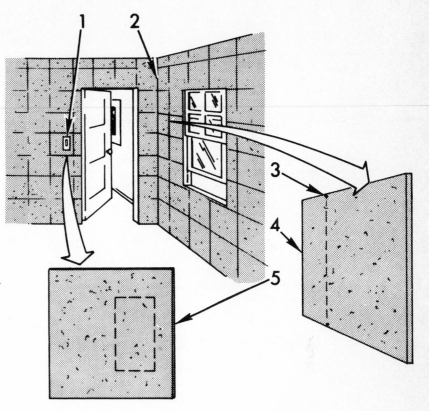

▶ **Installing Tiles**

Walls must be marked before you begin to install tiles. Page 43.

CAUTION

Be careful when handling cork tiles. Some grades of cork are extremely fragile and can crumble or break very easily.

During installation, tiles may have to be cut to fit along borders or around fixtures and obstacles. The preceding section (above) describes these procedures. Be sure to fit and cut each tile before applying adhesive or double-face tape.

First tile [1] is installed at 90° angle. If installing single vertical rows, first tile is butted against ceiling and aligned with plumb line [2].

Remaining tiles are installed in rows, using lines [2, 3] as a guide. Border tiles [4] requiring cutting can be installed last.

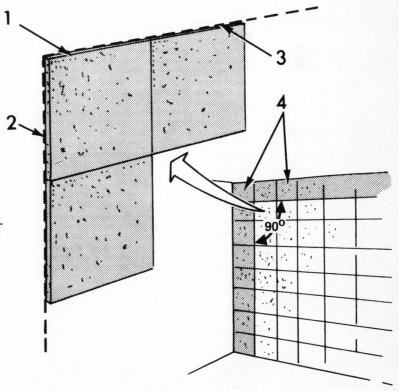

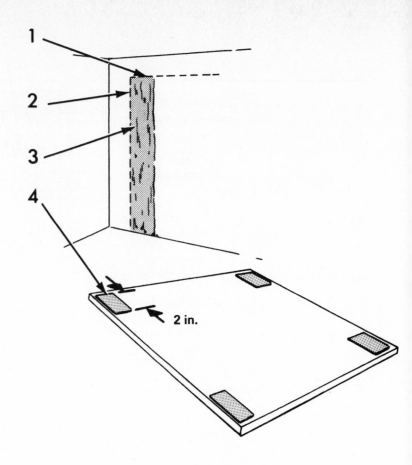

Installing Tiles

Tiles are installed with either adhesive or double-face tape. If using tape [4], apply it to the tiles in 2-inch strips and at 12-inch intervals.

Adhesive [3] is applied to the wall in tile-width strips. Read manufacturer's instructions for specific setup time as a guide for how much can be applied before installing tiles.

A notched trowel is used to apply adhesive. Do not cover lines [1, 2].

When using double-face tape [4], relocating tiles is very difficult. Be sure to install each tile in its correct position the first time.

For adhesives [3], relocation is somewhat easier. However, be careful not to slide tiles into position.

Installing Tiles

After cork tiles are installed, you may want to install molding [1] along tile borders. Molding may be an attractive addition to your wall covering, as well as a protection for tile edges.

If molding [1] is desired, go to Page 2 for a description of styles and applications of wood molding.

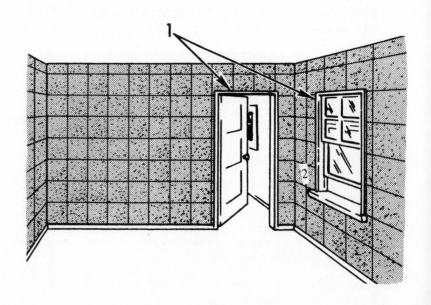

▶ Planning and Estimating

Planning for installation of mirror tiles depends entirely on your own decorative abilities and preferences. The variety of uses for mirror tile is almost endless.

You may decide to cover all walls in a room or just a single wall, or make mirror strips spaced at intervals of your own choosing. Mirror murals are available to add decorative touches to any room.

Regardless of how you decide to use mirror tiles, estimate the amount of tiles and double-face tape by performing the following steps:

1. Make a scale drawing of the surfaces to be covered. Include any fixtures and obstacles (doors, windows) not to be covered.

2. Take the drawing to the dealer. He will tell you the number of tiles and amount of double-face tape required.

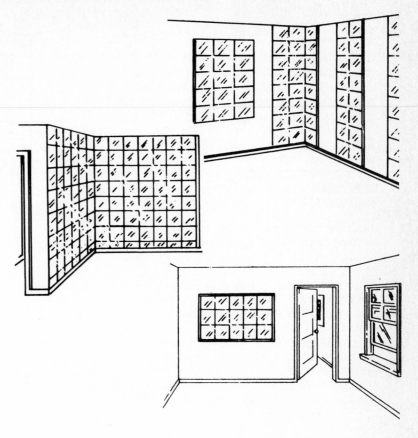

▶ Tools and Supplies

The following tools and supplies are required to install mirror tiles:

- A flexible metal rule [1] to measure areas to be tiled

- A straightedge [2] to aid in cutting tiles in straight lines. A metal edge is recommended, but any straight object can be used.

- A glass cutter [3] to cut tiles

- A grease pencil [4] to mark tiles for cutting

- A carpenter's square [5] to mark a 90° angle for first tile installed

- A plumb [6] to give a true, straight vertical line as a guide for installing tiles. A plumb can be constructed of a piece of string, some colored chalk, and any object suitable for a weight.

- Scissors [7] to cut double-face tape, if required

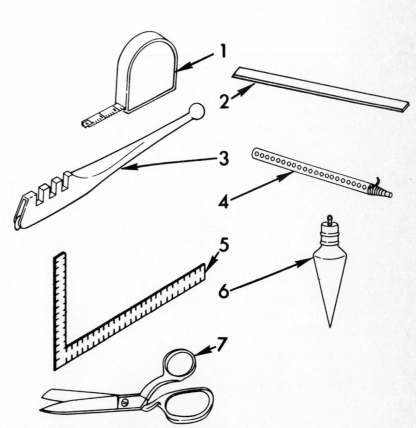

MIRROR TILES

▶ **Marking the Wall**

Having decided the application and pattern of your tile installation, you must mark a 90° angle on the wall as a guide for installing tiles. This ensures that all tiles are installed squarely on the wall, with all seams straight and even.

Wall surfaces must be prepared before marking the wall. Page 42.

A 90° angle is made with a plumb line [3] and chalk line [1].

Read the following paragraphs to determine where to mark the 90° angle for your specific application.

If installing tiles in a small area [2], such as for a mural, make the 90° angle at one corner of the area. Go to Page 49, Step 1 to mark the wall.

If installing tiles on an entire wall [5], or in vertical rows [4] which reach the ceiling, several considerations must be made to determine where to make the 90° angle. Go to next section (below).

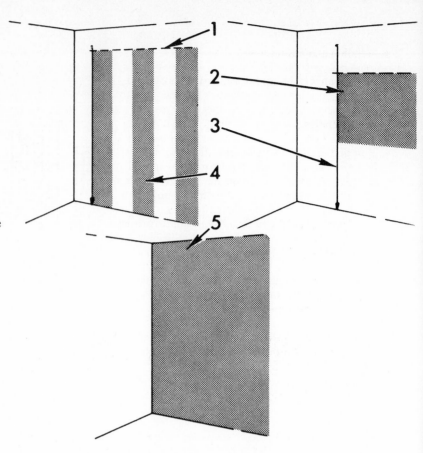

Marking the Wall

For single vertical rows of tiles [2], no 90° angle is needed. A plumb line [1] is made at the edge of each row. Go to Page 49, Step 2 to mark the plumb line.

For adjacent vertical rows of tiles [7], consider the following:

- The ceiling may not be exactly straight. Make several measurements from floor to ceiling to determine the lowest point [5] along the ceiling.

- Chalk line [6] is made at a distance of one tile [4] from the lowest point [5]. This prevents having to cut small strips of tile to fit irregularities.

- Tiles at high points [3] may leave gaps between ceiling and tiles. Gaps can be easily covered with decorative molding.

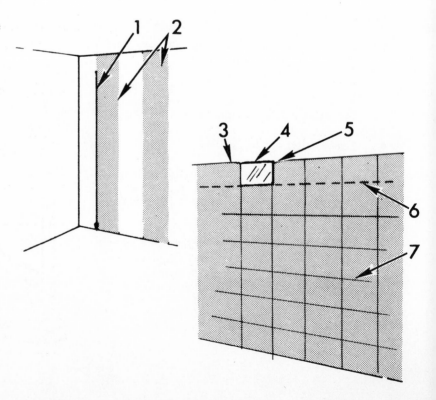

Marking the Wall

For tiling the entire width of a wall, the considerations for adjacent rows of tiles on Page 48 apply. In addition, consider the following:

- Corners may not be exactly straight. Make several measurements along the wall to determine its narrowest point [3].

- Plumb line [2] is made at a distance of one tile [4] from narrowest point [3]. This prevents having to cut small strips of tile to fit irregularities.

- Tiles at wide points [1] may leave gaps between corner and tiles. Gaps can be easily covered with decorative corner molding.

Perform the following steps to mark the 90° angle on the wall:

1. Determine location of 90° angle.

2. At desired location, mark a plumb line [7]. Page 13 describes how to mark a plumb line.

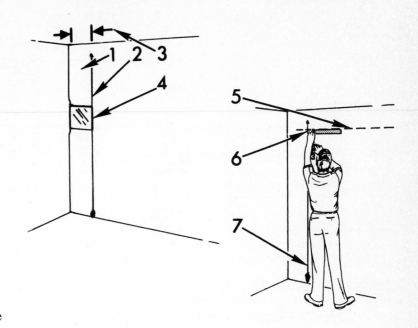

3. Using chalk and carpenter's square [6], mark a 90° angle to plumb line [7].

4. Extend chalk line [5] as required for your installation.

▶ **Cutting Tiles**

Mirror tiles may require cutting to fit around fixtures [1], or around ceiling and wall borders [2] or obstacles such as doors and windows.

For fixtures [1], remove the fixture cover. Measure and mark the tile [5] with a grease pencil to match the wall opening.

For ceiling and wall borders [2], and for obstacles, measure and mark the tile [4] according to the space to be covered.

Perform the following steps to cut the tile:

1. Align straightedge with marks [3] if required.

2. Using glass cutter, cut tile.

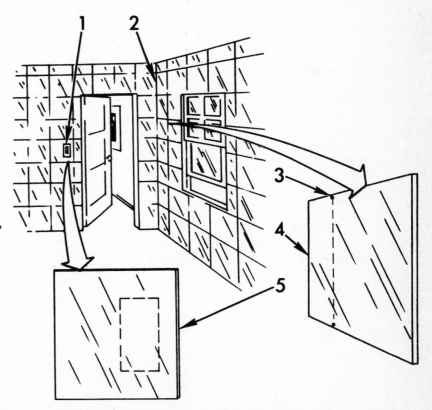

49

▶ **Installing Tiles**

Walls must be marked before you begin to install tiles. Page 48.

CAUTION

Be careful when handling mirror tiles. Some grades of mirror are extremely fragile and can break very easily, resulting in personal injury.

During installation, tiles may have to be cut to fit along borders or around fixtures and obstacles. Page 49 describes these procedures. Be sure to fit and cut each tile before applying double-face tape.

First tile [1] is installed at 90° angle. If installing single vertical rows, first tile is butted against ceiling and aligned with plumb line [2].

Remaining tiles are installed in rows, using lines [2, 3] as a guide. Border tiles [4] which require cutting can be installed last.

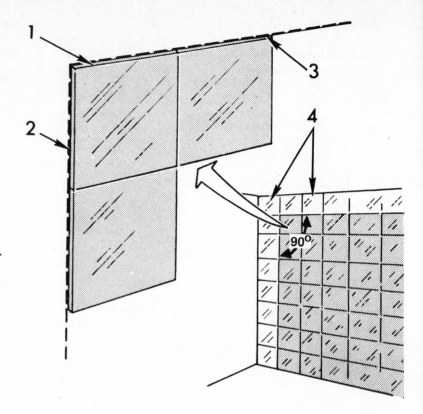

Installing Tiles

Tiles are installed with double-face tape [1]. Some tiles may have tape already installed. If applying tape, apply it in 2-inch strips at each corner.

Relocating tiles is difficult with double-face tape. Be sure to install each tile in its correct position the first time.

After mirror tiles are installed, you may want to install molding [2] along tile borders. Molding may be an attractive addition to your wall covering.

If molding [2] is desired, go to Page 2 for a description of styles and applications of wood molding.

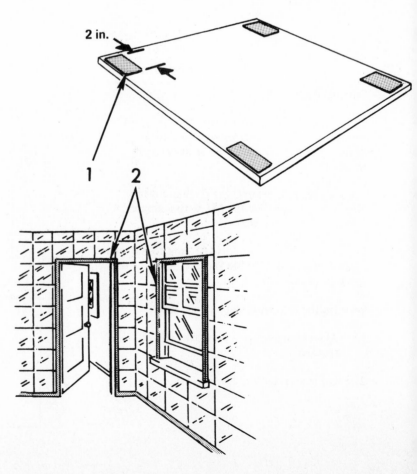

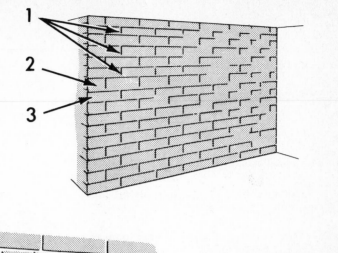

▶ Planning and Estimating

Planning for installation of simulated bricks depends on choosing the type of pattern you want and determining the quantity of required materials for that pattern.

Several patterns used in actual brickwork are shown in the illustration. Notice that vertical joints [1] in each row of brick are rarely directly above vertical joints in adjacent rows.

In most brick installations, alternate rows begin with whole bricks [3] and half bricks [2] to achieve proper spacing of vertical joints [1].

The patterns of whole, half, or quarter bricks depends entirely on your own preferences. However, all bricks are bought in whole sizes so more cutting is required for fractional sizes.

Planning and Estimating

Regardless of the pattern, bricks laid end to end [1] are called stretchers. Bricks laid side by side and turned vertically [2] are called headers.

Headers [2] are usually installed at tops of windows, doors, and fireplaces. Consider using headers along the floor line [3]. This application helps conceal any irregularities where floor and wall meet.

Estimate the amount of materials required for your purpose by performing the following steps:

1. Make a scale drawing of the surfaces to be covered. Include any fixtures and obstacles (doors, windows) not to be covered.

2. Take the drawing to the dealer. Keep in mind the pattern you want.

3. The dealer will tell you the amount of bricks and adhesive required. Also, ask him about a brick sealer.

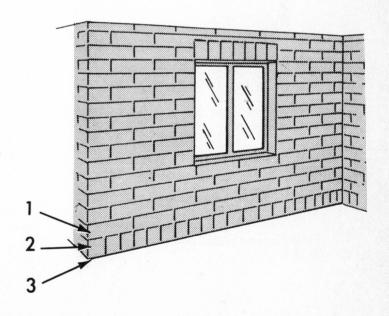

SIMULATED BRICKS

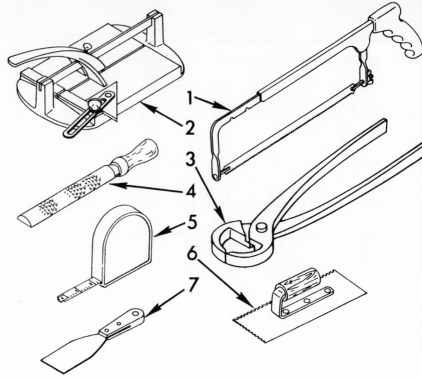

▶ **Tools and Supplies**

The following tools and supplies are required to install simulated bricks:

- A hacksaw [1] or coping saw to cut bricks. For ceramic bricks, a tile cutter [2] and tile nippers [3] are required.

- A common file [4] or rasp to file cut edges smooth

- A flexible metal rule [5] or ruler to measure brick sizes and areas to be covered

- A notched trowel [6] to apply adhesive to wall surfaces

- A 2-inch putty knife [7] to apply adhesive to bricks

Tools and Supplies

- A length of 3/8-inch dowel [1] to ensure correct spacing between bricks

- A carpenter's level [2] to ensure each row of bricks is installed exactly horizontal

- Clean rags to wipe adhesive from installed bricks

- Masking tape to protect surrounding surfaces while applying adhesive

- Drop cloths to protect floors while installing bricks

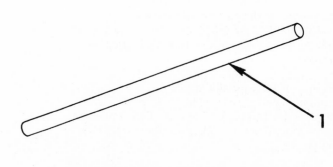

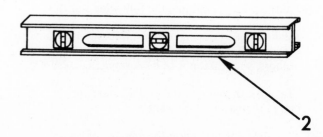

▶ Cutting Bricks

Simulated bricks may require cutting to fit around fixtures [1] and along ceiling and wall borders [2]. Depending on the pattern, half bricks and quarter bricks may be required in each row.

For fixtures [1], remove the fixture cover. Measure and mark the brick to match the wall opening.

For ceiling and wall borders [2], and for obstacles, measure and mark the brick according to the space to be covered.

When marking the brick for cutting, remember to allow for the 3/8-inch joint [3] between bricks and along borders, if required.

Most bricks [4], except ceramic bricks, are easily cut using a hacksaw or coping saw. The cut edge is then filed smooth with a common file or rasp.

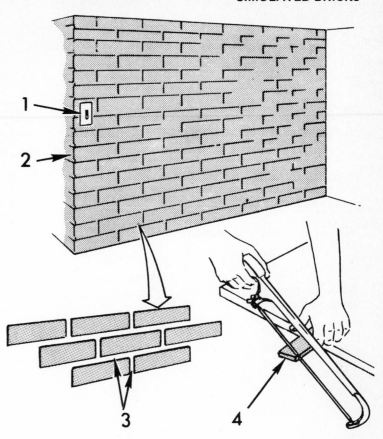

Cutting Bricks

To cut ceramic bricks [1], a tile cutter and nippers are required. Irregular cuts around fixtures and lengthwise cuts require tile nippers, using them to remove small pieces at a time. File edges smooth.

A tile cutter is used to cut ceramic bricks as follows:

1. Place brick [1] face down in the tile cutter. Score back of brick at location of cut.

2. Break scored brick [2] over a piece of dowel or other edge.

3. Using common file or rasp, smooth cut edges of brick [2].

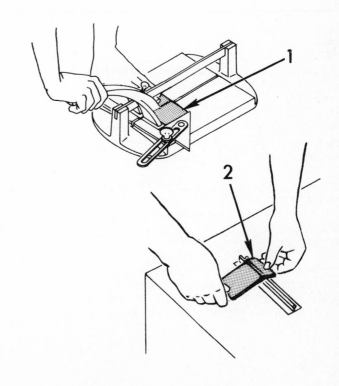

► Installing Bricks

Installation of simulated bricks is easy if you work slowly and carefully. Read this entire section before you begin.

Depending on your plans, you may want to remove baseboards and molding. Page 10. If not removing baseboards and molding, protect their finish with masking tape.

Wall surfaces must be prepared before installing bricks. Page 42.

Cover the floors in the work area with drop cloths. This will prevent adhesive from spattering on floor surfaces.

Bricks are installed in rows along entire width of area to be covered. Rows are installed from the floor up, following your chosen pattern.

Installing Bricks

A 3/8-inch space [4] must be maintained between each brick and along floor line [5] and borders [1].

When installation continues onto an adjoining wall, a 3/8-inch space [3] is allowed at every other row to provide a professional appearance.

Before beginning, read manufacturer's instructions for specific setup time of the adhesive. Use this as a guide for how much adhesive to apply and how many bricks to install at a time. Your working speed will also help determine this.

Begin by laying out 3 to 5 rows of bricks [2] along area to be covered. Arrange bricks for appearance and cutting requirements. Remember the 3/8-inch spaces [4] between bricks and along borders [1, 5].

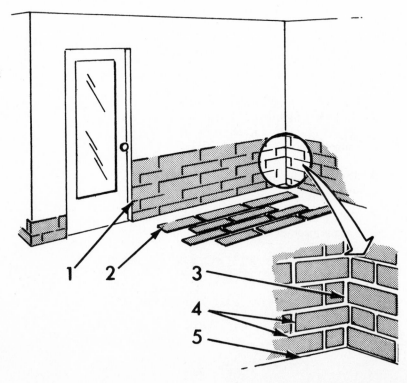

Installing Bricks

Page 53 describes cutting procedures. All cutting and arranging must be done before adhesive is applied.

Adhesive [1] is applied to wall in an area as recommended by the manufacturer. Use a notched trowel held at a right angle to spread adhesive evenly onto wall. Thickness should be 1/16- to 1/8-inch.

Adhesive must also be applied to the back of each brick. Use a putty knife to apply the following amounts:

Whole brick [3]: 3 spots, 1/8-inch thick,
    1-inch diameter
Half brick [4]: 1 spot, 1/8-inch thick,
    1-1/2 inch diameter
Quarter brick [5]: 1 spot, 1/8-inch thick,
    1-inch diameter

Install the first brick [2]. Do not slide brick into place. Press firmly so that all edges of brick are embedded in adhesive.

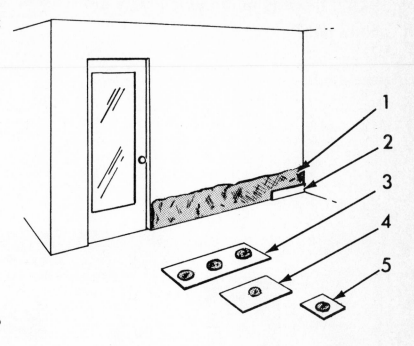

Installing Bricks

Install entire row of bricks [2]. Use a 3/8-inch dowel to insure correct spacing. Move the dowel along the spaces [1] to smooth adhesive.

After row of bricks [2] is installed, use a damp cloth to wipe any adhesive from face of bricks. Try not to move bricks when cleaning.

Use a carpenter's level to check that bricks [3] are level. Reposition bricks as required.

Repeat the process for each row of bricks [4] until job is complete: Apply adhesive, install bricks, space, clean and level as you go.

Follow manufacturer's instructions for drying time of the brick installation. When it is dry, apply brick sealer if desired.

What could be a more natural setting for simulated bricks than a fireplace? And if there is no fireplace, why not build one?

Transforming this room into a replica of early-day America is Z-BRICK's "Country Rustic Red," which has the rugged look of handmade brick. The traditional-style fireplace in this kitchen/family room is built with a prefabricated metal firebox, framed with plywood and covered with fireproof facing brick. *Photo courtesy of Z-BRICK Company.* (below)

The perfect complement to a richly paneled room, this massive fireplace has been tiled to stunning effect with white Z-BRICK "Fieldstone." *Photo courtesy of Z-BRICK Company.* (right)

The bold, dramatic look of Z-BRICK's "Fieldstone" is particularly effective on large walls like the one surrounding this fireplace. The random shapes and sizes of the textured tiles ensure that the finished wall is unique. *Photo courtesy of Z-BRICK Company.* (far right)

The combination of paneling and "Fieldstone" tiles (available in white, gray, or brown) give a rustic touch to this contemporary setting. *Photo courtesy of Z-BRICK Company.* (bottom right)

Brick tiles make an easy-care covering for kitchen walls.

The natural look and feel of brick has been created on this kitchen wall by the Brick/Master system of applying mortar over templates or tape to achieve a tiled look. The process is described on page 61. *Photo courtesy of Brick/Master, a subsidiary of Wonder Brix, Inc.* (top)

The transition from kitchen utility to dining elegance is accomplished with ease by Z-BRICK's ''Country Rustic Smoke.'' *Photo courtesy of Z-BRICK Company.* (bottom)

Bedrooms and home offices benefit from the versatility of brick wall coverings.

One-brick-at-a-time application makes it possible for the do-it-yourselfer to create a variety of patterns: basketweave, stack bond, or the herringbone on this office wall. *Photo courtesy of Z-BRICK Company.* (left)

Contrasting with the smooth luster of brass headboard and velvet quilt, the rough texture of Z-BRICK tiles gives this bedroom wall the look of "exposed" brick. *Photo courtesy of Z-BRICK Company.* (below left)

An interesting counterpoint to the Z-BRICK wall is provided in this bedroom by RUFF-IT premixed and precolored acrylic sculpture coat. Available in six designer colors, RUFF-IT creates a richly sculptured texture and adds offsetting color to a brick wall. *Photo courtesy of Z-BRICK Company.* (below right)

Handsome arches built with plywood, hardboard, and brick tiles can be adapted to dozens of uses.

Making the most of a small space, these arches house bookshelves, a bar, and even a Franklin stove. The arches are faced with Z-BRICK "Country Rustic Red." *Photos courtesy of Z-BRICK Company.*

60

The brick look can be created without tiles.

An alternative to tile application is offered by the Brick/Master system, in which mortar is applied over a template to achieve a bricklike appearance and texture. Brick-shaped templates or tape strips are applied to the wall over a base coat of mortar. Then the brick-colored texturing compound is troweled over the template or tape to the desired thickness. The template or tape is removed, leaving the "bricks" outlined. *Photos courtesy of Brick/Master, a subsidiary of WonderBrix, Inc.*

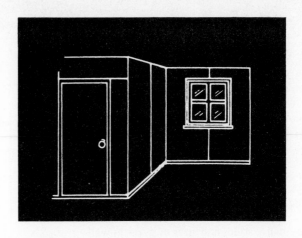

GYPSUM WALLBOARD PANELING

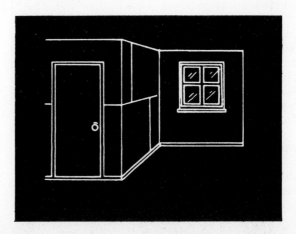

Gypsum wallboard panels are sometimes called other names such as drywall, SHEETROCK (a trademark of United States Gypsum) and plasterboard. They are more widely used for wall and ceiling coverings in new frame home construction than any other material.

Gypsum wallboard panels consist of a solid gypsum core [1] with a liner paper on the back side [2] and heavy, smooth finished paper on the front side [3].

There are many styles and sizes of gypsum wallboard to fit almost any construction need. However, there is one style better suited for use by the home pro than any other. It is the 4 ft by 8 ft sheet panel with two tapered edges [4]. These edges are slightly tapered for a distance [5] of about 2-1/2 inches. The ends [1] of the panel are not tapered. Also, unlike the tapered edges, they are not covered with paper.

Wallboard panels are available in 3/8-in., 1/2-in., and 5/8-in. thicknesses. Because wallboard is very heavy to handle, the home pro may wish to use the thinnest sheet possible for his purposes. In many localities, the thickness required is specified by building codes. For example, walls between a home and an attached garage may require 5/8-in. thick panels; 3/8-in. minimum thickness may be specified for downstairs interior walls, and 1/2-in. minimum thickness for use in upstairs rooms of two-story homes. Check your local building codes before selecting your panels.

Most wallboard is installed on framing constructed of 2 x 4 studs spaced at 16-inch intervals between centers. However, some homes may have studs spaced at 20-inch or 24-inch intervals. If studs are spaced more than 16 inches apart, wallboard panels of at least 1/2-inch thickness are required.

If wallboard panels are to be installed on furring strips, it is generally a good idea to use 2 x 2 furring strips rather than the smaller sizes. Furring strips should be spaced at 16-inch intervals between centers.

All procedures for wallboard installation in this book are based upon installation of 4 ft by 8 ft panels on wood framing with studs spaced at 16-inch intervals. If your situation is different, slight changes in procedures may be required. It is also assumed that rough wiring and plumbing is installed.

Wallboard panels may be attached by any of three methods: nails, adhesive and nails, or screws. Although all methods will be described, the easiest method for the home pro to use is probably nailing.

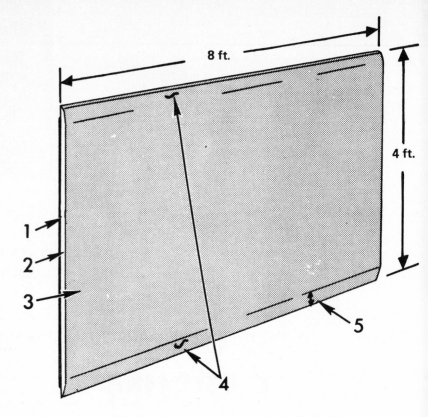

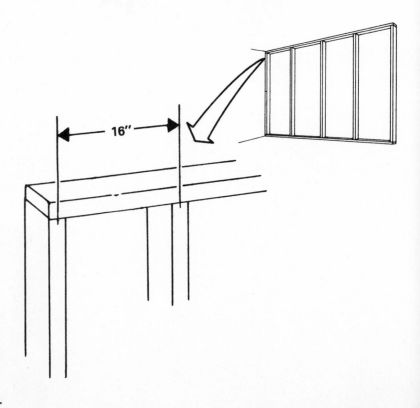

▶ Tools

A number of common tools and some special-purpose tools are required to do a professional-looking job. The special tools are relatively inexpensive and should be obtained to ensure good results.

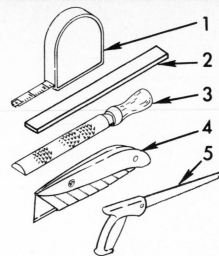
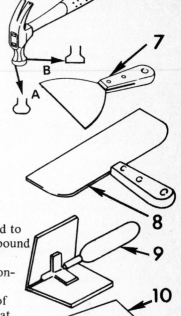

Measuring tape [1]

Straightedge [2]. Length should be 4 feet. Although a metal edge is preferred, any straight length of board or furring will do.

Rasp [3] or coarse grit sandpaper

Utility knife [4]

Keyhole saw [5]

Crown head hammer [6] or wallboard hammer. It is necessary to use a hammer with a crown head [A] rather than a flat head [B]. The sharp edges of a flat head will tear and damage the paper surface of wallboard when used to drive nails.

4-inch joint finishing knife [7]

10-inch joint finishing knife [8]

Corner tool [9]

Mortar board [10]. Mortar board is used to carry and hold a supply of joint compound while working. It can be constructed from scrap wood. Carrying surface consists of a smooth, flat board about 8 inches by 12 inches in size. Edges of board must be smooth and even so that blade of joint finishing knife can be scraped against it to remove excess joint compound from blade while working. Handle can be made of 2 x 4 scrap.

▶ Supplies

Procedures for estimating quantity of supplies are given in Planning and Estimating, Page 66.

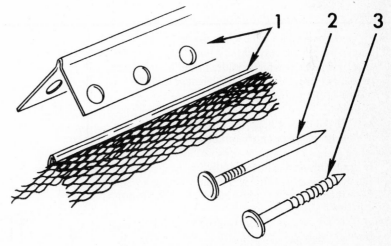

4 ft by 8 ft sheets of gypsum wallboard with tapered edges. Thickness as required.

All-purpose joint compound (cement). Be sure to specify all-purpose compound. Many kinds of special-purpose joint compounds are available to fit all construction needs. However, all-purpose compound is best suited for the home pro. It can be used for all patching and cementing purposes. In addition, it can be used to texture the completed walls and ceilings. Consult your dealer about purchasing premixed or powdered compound. The best choice for you depends on the size and duration of your job.

Joint tape. A non-adhesive paper tape.

Corner beads [1]. These are inexpensive, lightweight metal angles which are used rather than joint tape. They provide a smooth, even edge to corners. They protect otherwise exposed edges of wallboard from damage. They are used on outside

corners of walls, around casement windows, corners of columns, and around large doorways of other wall openings.

Gypsum panel nails. Heads are slightly concave to hold cement and reduce chances of tearing wallboard paper. Two types of nails are available: cement coated nails [2] and annular ring nails [3]. Consult your dealer to determine the best type and size nail for your particular job.

Supplies

Screws, if desired. Special screws are used for installing gypsum wallboard panels. Many styles are available to fit all construction needs. Consult your dealer to determine the specific style and length screw required for your particular job.

Power-driven screwdrivers with special heads are required for installing screws.

Adhesive, if desired. Special adhesive is available for attaching gypsum wallboard panels to wood framing or furring strips. Adhesive is applied with a cartridge gun.

Adhesive is used in combination with nails. Use of adhesive results in about a 75% reduction in the number of nails required when nails alone are used. Also, panels are bonded more strongly to the framing than when nails alone are used. However, it is unlikely that the home pro will find this method of attachment advantageous for limited application.

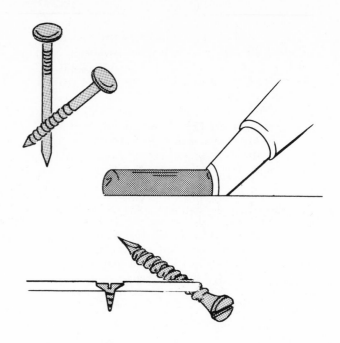

■■■ **PLANNING AND ESTIMATING** ■■■

Gypsum wallboard panels may be arranged vertically [1] or horizontally [2] on walls. Select the arrangement which results in the least number of joints. In general, this will be accomplished by applying the following rules:

● If the ceiling height is 8 ft 2 in. or less, arrange panels horizontally.

If arranging panels horizontally, try stagger end (butt) joints [3]. This will make them less visible than if they are aligned to make an 8 foot joint.

● If the ceiling height is more than 8 ft 2 in., arrange panels vertically.

● If a wall is 4 ft wide or less, apply the panel vertically.

On ceilings, panels can be arranged so that they are lengthwise with the joists [4] or so that they go across the joists [5]. Select the arrangement which results in the fewest joints between panels. Stagger end (butt) joints if possible.

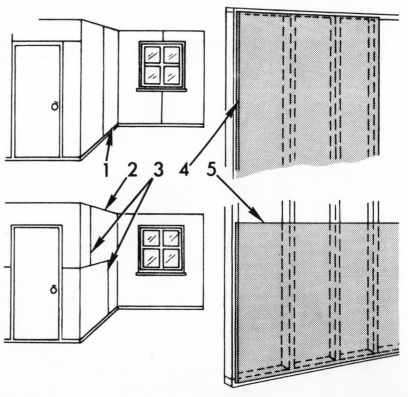

To estimate number of panels required:

1. Determine area (square feet) of each surface to be covered.

2. Add all areas to obtain total area.

3. Determine areas of large picture windows and large doorways. Do not determine areas of standard sized windows and doorways. The scrap wallboard from these small openings usually can not be used elsewhere.

4. Subtract area determined in Step 3 from total area.

5. Divide area determined in Step 4 by 32 to estimate total number of 4 ft by 8 ft panels required.

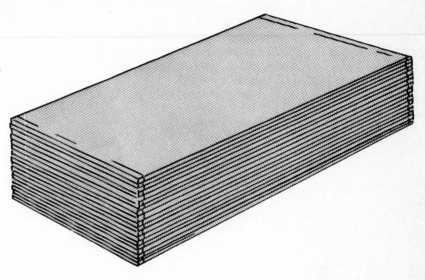

Panels can be stored flat or on edge. Panels are very heavy. Be sure not to stack so many panels in one place that floor joists are in danger of breaking.

If panels are stacked, stack can serve as work surface for measuring and cutting panels.

To estimate amount of joint tape and joint compound, use the following chart:

Area of Surface (from Step 4)	Ready Mixed Compound	Dry Compound	Joint Tape
200 sq ft	1 gal.	12 lbs	120 ft
400 sq ft	2 gals.	24 lbs	180 ft
600 sq ft	3 gals.	36 lbs	250 ft
800 sq ft	4 gals.	48 lbs	310 ft
1000 sq ft	5 gals.	60 lbs	370 ft

To estimate size and quantities of nails, use the following chart:

Wallboard Thickness	Size of Nail* Cement Coated	Size of Nail* Annular Ring	Quantity per 1000 sq ft
3/8 in.	1 5/8 in.	1 1/4 in.	5 1/4 lbs
1/2 in.	1 5/8 in.	1 1/4 in.	5 1/4 lbs
5/8 in.	1 7/8 in.	1 3/8 in.	6 3/4 lbs; 5 1/4 lbs

*For applying directly to wood framing

If using adhesives or screws, consult with dealer to determine selection and quantity required for your application.

PLANNING AND ESTIMATING

It is recommended that corner beads [4] be installed on all outside corners in the room.

Corner beads are usually available in 8 foot lengths. Scrap pieces from around windows or other openings usually cannot be used elsewhere because sections of corner beads should not be joined. Corner beads should be installed in single, unjointed lengths if possible.

Corner beads [4] should be installed

- at exposed edges [1] of large doorways

- at exposed edges [2] of casement windows

- at outside corners [3] of walls

- at edges of columns, soffits or other enclosures.

To estimate number of corner beads required, count number of outside corners in room.

Determine number of complete lengths of corner beads required to cover all outside corners.

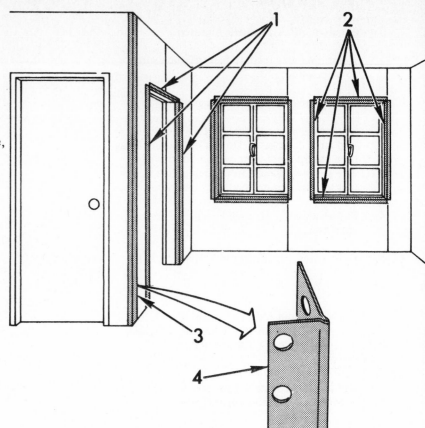

◼ MEASURING AND CUTTING ◼

▶ **Measuring and Cutting Sections of Panels**

Gypsum wallboard panels must never be forced into position. Therefore, all measurements must allow for loose fits between panels or sections of panels.

Fits between panels or sections can range from firm contact (as along the joint between a wall and ceiling) up to 1/4-inch gaps.

If gaps are less than 1/4-inch, it is not necessary to fill gaps before taping.

If gaps are 1/4-inch or more, they must be filled before taping them.

Most corners are slightly out of plumb. Therefore, two measurements [1] should be made at corners before marking [2] and cutting panel.

When measuring panels, try to arrange panels so that sections are at least 8 inches wide.

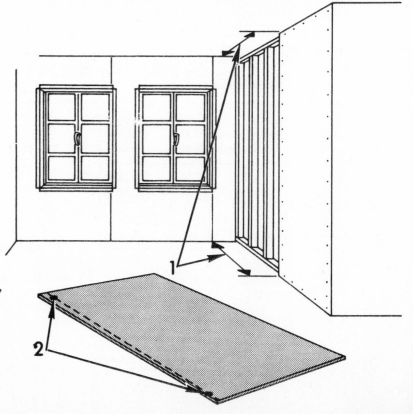

Measuring and Cutting Sections of Panels

Arrange panels so that joints are butt to butt [1] or tapered edge to tapered edge [2]. Do not place an untapered (butt) edge next to a tapered edge [3].

If you can arrange panels so that butt joints are staggered [4], these joints will be easier to conceal.

Before cutting panel, be sure that all ends and edges which run lengthwise with joists or studs are supported by joists or studs. Ends and edges which are at right angles to framing need not be supported.

1. Measure and mark panel in two places [5].

2. Using straightedge and knife, cut through layer of paper into gypsum core of panel. Use enough pressure to cut slightly into core.

3. Break panel at cut [6] by bending.

4. Cut through paper [7].

5. Using rasp or coarse sandpaper on block of wood, smooth edge of section.

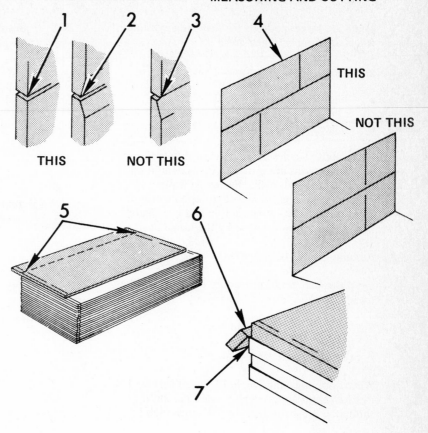

THIS NOT THIS

THIS

NOT THIS

▶ **Making Cutouts**

Cutouts for window and door openings are generally made after panel is installed.

Cutouts for electrical outlets are made before the panel is installed. They are made as follows:

1. Place and hold panel at installed position.

2. Using hammer and block of wood, tap on panel at approximate location of outlet. Tap panel hard enough so that outlet box makes an impression [1] on backing paper of panel.

3. Remove panel and position it so that impression [1] is face up.

4. Using drill, make holes at corners of impression [1].

5. Using keyhole saw, make cutout.

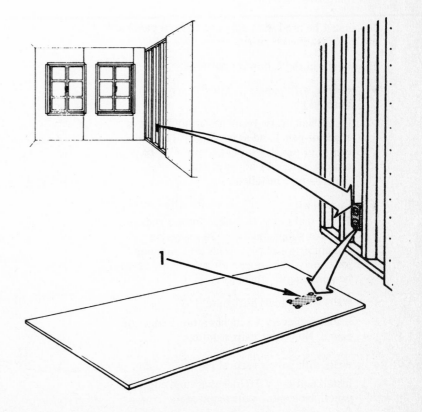

There are three methods for fastening gypsum wallboard panels. They are:

- Fastening with Adhesive/Nails, Page 70.

- Fastening with Screws, Page 71.

- Fastening with Nails, Page 72.

Each method is described. Detailed procedures and illustrations are provided for fastening wallboard panels with nails. Fastening wallboard with nails has long been the most common method used in residential construction and is probably best suited for application by the home pro.

▶ **Fastening with Adhesive/Nails**

Read through entire procedure before installing panels.

Surfaces must be clean and free of grease.

Area must be well ventilated.

When applying adhesive, hold gun so that tip [2] of cartridge is at 45 degree angle [3]. Bead [1] should be 3/8-inch wide and 3/8-inch high [1].

Begin applying bead 6 inches from end of stud or joist and finish bead 6 inches from other end.

Moving gun at constant speed, apply bead in continuous length [4]. If applying bead on stud or joist where panels meet, use zig-zag pattern [5].

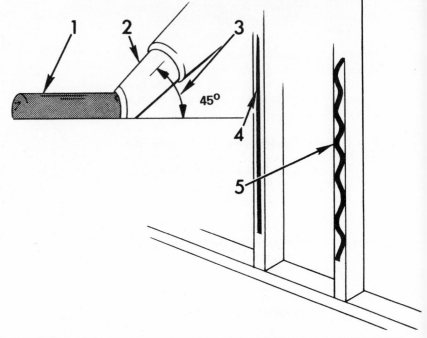

Fastening with Adhesive/Nails

Nails must be used with adhesive to hold panel in place while adhesive dries.

Space nails in the following patterns:

- **Ceiling with panels lengthwise across joists [1]**

  Install nail every 16 inches around ends or edges of panel and at every joist [2] along center of panel. Nails at center may be removed after 48 hours or may be permanently installed.

- **Ceiling with panels lengthwise with joists [3]**

  Install nail every 16 inches around ends or edges of panel and every 24 inches on remaining joists [4]. Nails on remaining joists may be removed after 48 hours or may be permanently installed.

- **Walls with panels horizontal [5]**

  Install nail every 16 inches around edges of panel. No center nails required.

- **Walls with panels vertical [6]**

  Install nail every 16 inches around edges of panel. No center nails required.

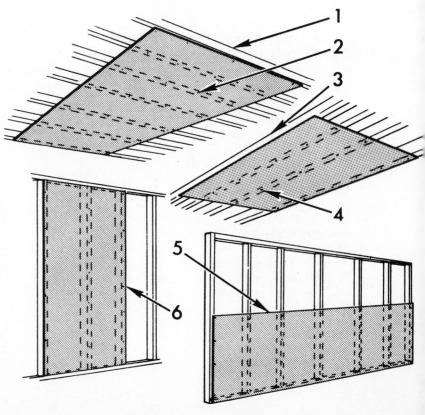

Fastening with Adhesive/Nails

When applying adhesive to studs or joists, do not apply adhesive beyond area panel will cover.

1. Apply beads [1] of adhesive to studs or joists.

2. Place panel [2] at installed position.

When installing nails begin at center of panel and work to edges.

Nails must not be placed closer to ends or edges of panel than 3/8-inch.

If nail is to be installed permanently, drive nail so that head is 1/32-inch below surface [3] of panel. Dent [4] will be seen. Paper must not be torn. If paper is torn, remove nail and install another nail 1-1/2 inches from damaged area.

If nail is to be removed after adhesive dries, use spacer made of scrap wallboard between nail and panel.

3. Install nails.

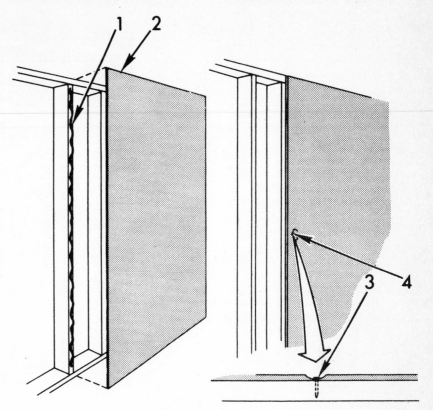

▶ **Fastening with Screws**

Read through entire procedure before installing panels. Space screws in the following patterns:

*   Ceilings [1]

    Maximum space between screws on all joists is 12 inches.

*   Walls [2]

    Maximum space between screws on all studs is 16 inches.

Screws must not be placed closer to ends or edges of panel than 3/8-inch.

Adjustable depth control of power screwdriver head must be set so that head of screw is driven 1/32-inch below surface [3] of panel. Paper must not be torn when installing screw.

1. Place panel at installed position.

When using power screwdriver, keep it operating constantly. Automatic clutch disengages driver head when screw is properly set. Remove screwdriver from screw instantly when head is disengaged.

Screw must be installed perpendicular to surface.

2. **While holding panel, install screws.**

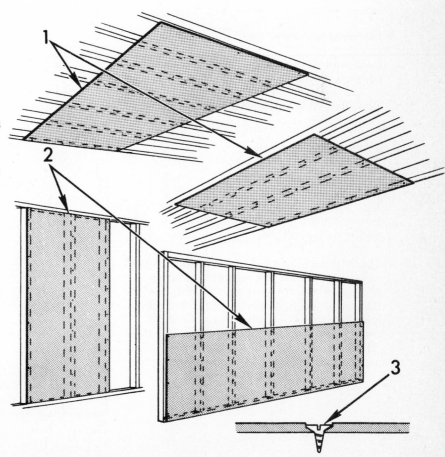

Fastening panels with screws. *Photo courtesy of United States Gypsum Company.*

▶ **Fastening with Nails**

Read through entire procedure before installing panels.

Two methods of spacing nails are commonly used. They are the:

● Single nailing method

● Double nailing method

The single nailing method is most commonly used. However, there is a slight advantage in using the double nailing method.

The double nailing method reduces the frequency of loose panels due to improper installation. If the panel has not been pushed firmly against the stud or joist while installing the first nail, it is likely that this error will be noticed and corrected during installation of the second nail. This is the main advantage of the double nailing method over the single nailing method.

Nailing Patterns

Single Nailing Method	Double Nailing Method
Ceilings: Install nails at all joists. Space nails at 7-inch intervals.	Ceilings: Install nails at all joists. Space nails on edges of panel at 7-inch intervals. Single nail only. Space nails on all other joists at 12-inch intervals. Install a second nail about 2-1/2 inches from first nail.
Walls: Install nails at all studs. Space nails at 8-inch intervals.	Walls: Install nails at all studs. Space nails on edges of panel at 8-inch intervals. Single nail only. Space nails on all other studs at 12-inch intervals. Install a second nail about 2-1/2 inches from first nail.

Fastening with Nails

Nails should not be spaced closer to edges or ends than 3/8-in. If nails are closer, gypsum core can easily be damaged when driving nail head into panel.

Nails at joints [1] should be placed opposite each other.

When driving nail, be sure to hold nail perpendicular to panel. Nail must not be installed at an angle.

While driving nail, push and hold panel firmly against stud or joist. Never rely on the nail to pull the panel against the stud or joist.

Begin nailing at center of panel and work to edges.

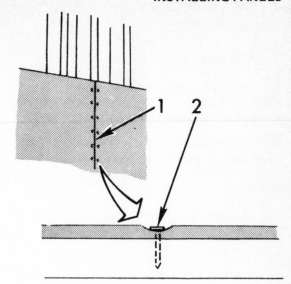

1. Place panel at installed position.

2. While holding panel firmly against framing, drive nail into panel until head of nail is flush with surface of panel.

3. Using crown head hammer, strike nail one time hard enough to drive head 1/32-inch below surface of panel [2].

If using double nailing method, check that first nail is still firmly in place after installing second nail.

If nail bends or paper surface of panel is torn, nail must be removed. Install new nail 1-1/2 inches from damaged area.

When installing gypsum wallboard panels, the ceiling must be paneled before walls.

▶ **Installing Panels on Ceilings**

Read through entire procedure before installing panels.

When positioning panels, be sure that edges [1] or ends [2] which run lengthwise with joists are supported by joists. Edges [1] or ends [2] must be placed on center line of joist if joining other panels on joist.

Cutouts for ceiling fixtures must be accurately located and closely fitted.

Because they are not tapered, end (butt) joints [3] are the most difficult joints to conceal. Therefore stagger end joints [3] when possible to aid concealment.

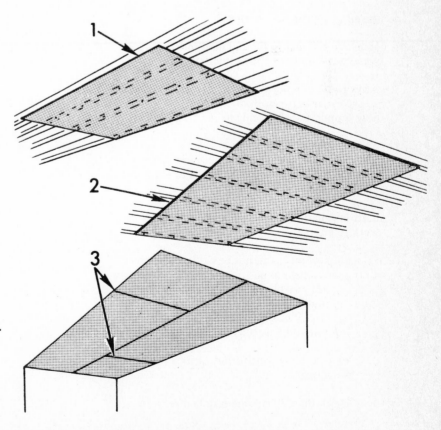

INSTALLING PANELS

Installing Panels on Ceiling

Two persons are required to install panels on ceilings. Teamwork and technique is required to make this difficult task easier.

The task of holding the panel in position is made much easier if your helper is equipped with a T-bar. A T-bar is constructed from wood as follows:

1. Measure distance from floor to ceiling. Add 2 inches to distance.

2. Using 1 in. x 4 in. or similar stock, cut a board to length determined in Step 1.

3. Cut a 3 foot length of board. Top of edge of board must be smooth and even to prevent damage to surface of panel.

4. Construct a T-bar by nailing lengths of board together [1].

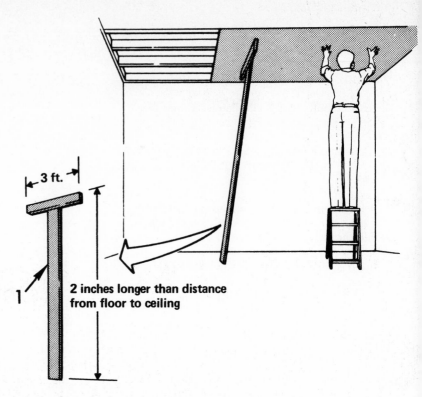

3 ft.

2 inches longer than distance from floor to ceiling

Installing Panels on Ceilings

Helper uses T-bar to lift and hold one end of panel while home pro lifts other end of panel.

After panel is in position against joists, helper can wedge T-bar between floor and panel. T-bar can now support panel, freeing helper to do other tasks.

While holding panel in position against joists with his head, home pro uses both hands to place and drive nails into panel.

Start installation of nails at center of panel and work to edges.

If location of joists can not be easily determined after panel is held in position, it may be necessary to first mark panel with pencil lines to indicate location of joists.

1. Measure and cut panel as required.

2. While holding panel firmly against joists, install nails.

3. Check that all nails are installed securely.

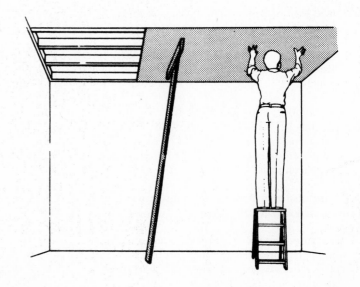

▶ **Installing Panels on Walls**

Read through entire procedure before installing panels.

When positioning panels, be sure that edges [3] or ends [4] which run lengthwise with studs are supported by studs. Edges [3] or ends [4] must be placed on center line of stud if joining other panels on stud.

Cutouts for wall fixtures must be accurately located and closely fitted.

Because they are not tapered, end (butt) joints [5] are the most difficult to conceal. Therefore, stagger end joints [5] when possible to aid concealment.

If installing panels on both sides of a partition, check that panels on one side of partition are not loosened by hammering on other side of partition.

Also, same stud should not be used for panel joints on both sides of partition.

If installing panels horizontally [1] on wall, go next section (below).

If installing panels vertically [2] on wall, go to Page 76.

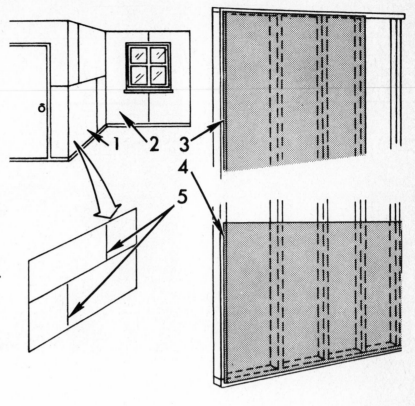

▶ **Installing Panels Horizontally on Walls**

Panels can be installed on walls by one person. By following these procedures, the task can be made easier.

Top panel [1] must be installed before bottom panel. Top panel [1] must be placed against ceiling panel [2].

1. At a distance of about 48-1/2 inches from ceiling, drive large nails [3] part way into two studs.

2. Lift panel [4] onto nails. Nails will support panel.

3. While lifting and holding one end of panel into installed position, drive a nail [5] through panel to hold panel in position.

4. Lift other end of panel into installed position and secure with a nail.

Be sure to push panel firmly against studs while nailing.

5. Working from center of panel to edges, install remaining nails.

6. Check that all nails are installed securely.

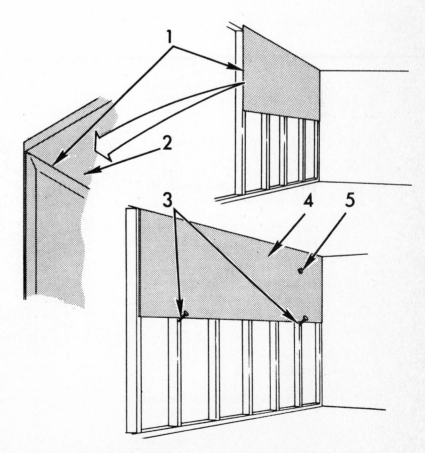

Installing panels of insulated sheathing—gypsum board horizontally on walls. Note cutouts for window openings and electrical outlets. *Photo courtesy of United States Gypsum Company.*

▶ **Installing Panels Vertically on Walls**

Panels can be installed on walls by one person. By following these procedures, the task can be made easier.

Panel [2] must be placed against ceiling panel [1].

1. While holding panel [4] at installed position, push two wedges [5] under panel [4]. Wedges will hold panel against ceiling.

2. While pushing top of panel against studs, install nails [3] at three places along top of panel. Nails will hold panel in position.

3. Remove wedges [5].

Be sure to push panel firmly against studs while nailing.

4. Working from center of panel to edges, install remaining nails.

5. Check that all nails are installed securely.

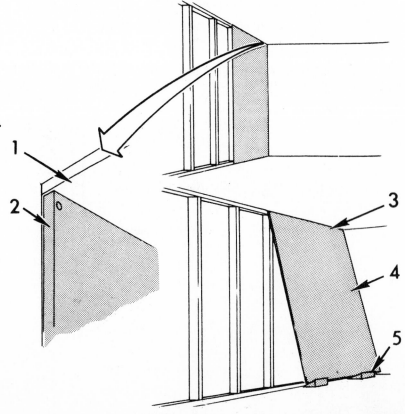

▶ Installing Corner Beads

Corner beads are installed at all exposed corners.

Corner beads should be of correct length.
To avoid joints in corner beads, do not use short
pieces of scrap corner bead to construct longer
lengths.

1.   Using tin shears, cut corner bead [2] to
      correct length.

Drywall nails [1] are spaced at 6-inch intervals.
They are installed on both sides of flange, directly
opposite each other.

2.   Place and hold corner bead [2] at installed
      position.

Nails are driven through metal, not into
pre-formed holes [3].

3.   Install nails. Nail heads are flush with
      surface of corner bead.

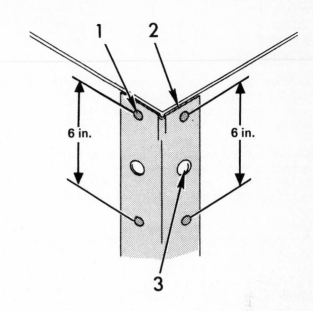

▶ Inspecting the Job

Entire installation should be inspected to ensure
that it is ready for taping and cementing.

If panels are installed on both sides of a partition,
be especially careful to check for panels that may
have been loosened by hammering.

1.   Push firmly against all panels to determine
      whether there is movement toward studs or
      joists. Drive in nails as required.

2.   Using 4-inch joint finishing knife [1], scrape
      over all nails. Metallic sound indicates nail
      head is not seated correctly. Drive in nails
      as required.

3.   Check all joints and fittings. Gaps 1/4-inch
      wide or larger must be filled with joint
      compound. Go to Page 79 for filling gaps.

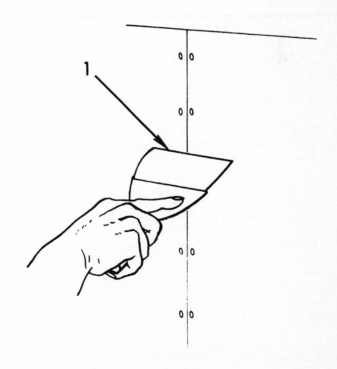

After panels are installed, all dents must be filled to provide a smooth surface. All joints must be taped and cemented.

The purpose of taping and cementing the panels is to provide a smooth, even surface for paint, wallpaper and other coverings.

The most difficult task for amateurs is to prepare the joints so that they are not visible after the ceilings and walls are painted or otherwise decorated.

Texture patterns and paints go a long way toward concealing the joints. However, they are no substitute for careful and correct taping and cementing. They will not hide poor-quality work.

Dents [1] and tapered edge joints [2] are relatively easy to fill smoothly. Joint compound is added until surface is smooth.

End or butt joints [3] are much more difficult to finish. The joint will necessarily be higher than the rest of the surface. The objective of taping and cementing is to apply and taper (feather) the joint compound [4] so smoothly and evenly that no shadows or edges are visible.

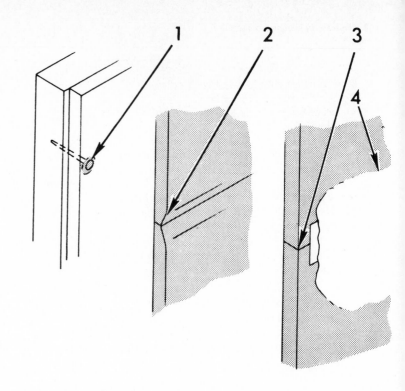

All joints require taping and cementing. All dents require cementing only. In both cases, cementing is a three-step job. It consists of:

- Applying the first coat [1]. Taping, if required, is accomplished during this step. Joint compound is applied to all joints and dents.

- Applying the second coat [2]. The purpose of this step is to apply a second layer of joint compound to all joints and dents to make the surface more smooth and even.

- Applying the third coat [3]. The purpose of this step is to apply a third layer of joint compound to all joints and dents. It is the final step in making the surface smooth and even.

You should try to apply each coat so smoothly and evenly that smoothing with sandpaper is almost unnecessary.

Before applying tape and joint compound to joints, all gaps 1/4-inch wide or larger must be filled. Go to Page 79 for filling gaps.

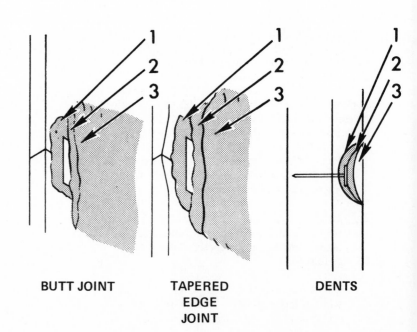

BUTT JOINT   **TAPERED EDGE JOINT**   **DENTS**

▶ Mixing Joint Compound

If using powdered compound, mix only as much as you need for the day. It is difficult to store well.

Always keep inside edges of container clean. If thin layer of joint compound dries and becomes mixed into rest of compound, it will cause lumps in compound. Never use compound with lumps. It cannot provide a smooth finish.

Container and mixing tools must be clean. Drinking-quality water must be used.

Read manufacturer's instructions for correct mixture of water and powder.

1. Add water to container.

2. Using 4-inch joint finishing knife, slowly sift powder into water. Allow powder to become thoroughly wet.

3. Stir mixture until evenly wet.

4. Allow to soak as required by manufacturer's instructions.

Consistency of compound is similar to peanut butter.

▶ Filling Gaps

All gaps 1/4-inch wide or larger must be filled.

If panels have been installed with adhesive, adhesive must be allowed to dry for 48 hours before filling gaps or taping joints.

If not using pre-mixed joint compound, mix amount of joint compound required for filling gaps. Joint compound may be mixed to consistency thicker than peanut butter. Go to preceding section (above) for mixing joint compound.

Joint finishing knife is held at 45 degree angle.

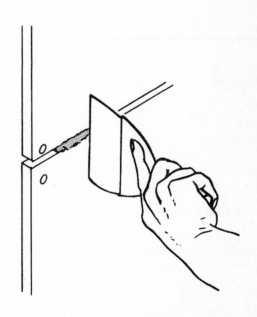

1. Using 4-inch joint finishing knife, force joint compound into gaps.

2. Smooth joint compound even with surface of panels.

3. Scrape all excess joint compound from surface of panels. Joint compound should be visible only in gaps and dents. It should not cover surface of panels.

4. Allow to dry 24 hours.

5. Check joint compound for cracks and shrinkage. Refill gaps as necessary to bring compound approximately even with surface of panels.

Applying the first coat of joint compound. *Photo courtesy of United States Gypsum Company.*

Before first coat is applied, all gaps 1/4-inch or larger must be filled. Page 79.

Read through entire procedure before applying first coat.

So that compound does not dry too fast, it may be necessary to reduce ventilation by keeping windows closed.

First coat is applied with 4-inch joint finishing knife.

▶ **Tapered-edge Joints and Butt Joints**

1. Apply band of joint compound [1] over joint. Band is approximately 1/8-in. thick and 4 inches wide.

When applying tape to joint, do not cross over tape at another joint. Only one layer of tape is used where joints meet or intersect [3].

Length of tape should be as long as you can easily handle — up to 8 feet or as required.

2. Tear length of tape from roll.

3. Press tape [2] into joint compound.

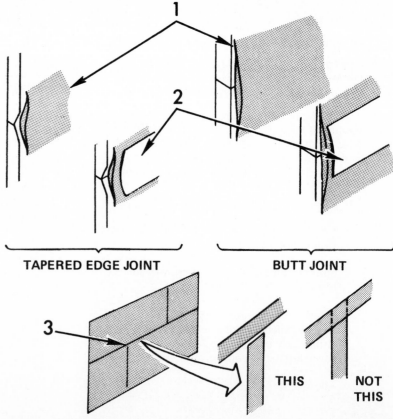

TAPERED EDGE JOINT   BUTT JOINT

THIS   NOT THIS

4. Holding knife at 45 degree angle, pull knife along tape [1] to press tape evenly into compound. Remove excess compound.

Pressure should be enough that:

*   Surface of tape is smooth and even and uncovered by compound.

*   Edges of tape are covered by compound.

*   1/32-inch of compound remains evenly spread under tape to bond tape to panels. If more compound is removed, tape may pull from joint when dry.

5. Using knife, cover tape with thin layer of compound [2].

    *   Layer of compound is sufficiently thin that tape may be visible through it.

    *   Layer is smooth and even. Edges of layer are feathered into panel smoothly so that no ridges or roughness can be seen or felt.

    *   Layer is 4 in. to 6 in. wide.

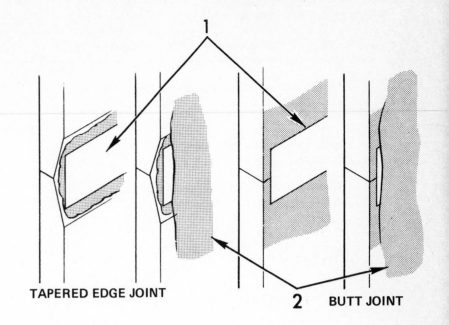

TAPERED EDGE JOINT

BUTT JOINT

6. Allow to dry 24 hours.

7. Smooth joint by sanding lightly with 220 grit sandpaper.

▶ **Inside Corner Joints**

Corner tool is held at about 30 degree angle.

1. Using corner tool, apply band of joint compound [1] to corner and surfaces of panels on both sides of corner. Practice using tool until you learn to spread compound evenly on both surfaces at same time.

2. Fold length of tape [2] into two equal widths.

3. Press tape [2] into joint compound.

Before doing Steps 4 and 5, read **Step 4 and 5** above for proper technique for embedding and covering tape.

4. Pull corner tool along tape [2] to press tape evenly into compound. Remove excess compound.

5. Using 4-inch joint finishing knife, cover one side [3] of tape with compound.

6. Cover other side [4] of tape with compound. Steps 5 and 6 may have to be repeated several times to obtain smooth and even surface.

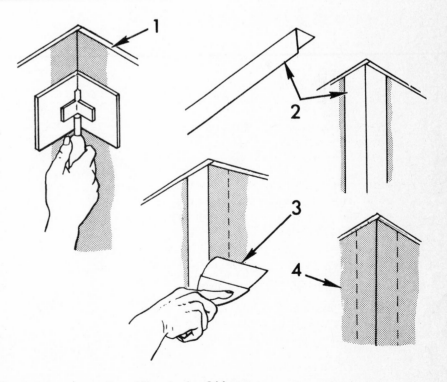

7. Allow to dry 24 hours.

8. Smooth joint by sanding lightly with 220 grit sandpaper.

APPLYING THE FIRST COAT

▶ **Outside Corner Joints**

Before applying joint compound, outside corners must have corner beads [1] installed.

1. Using 4-inch joint finishing knife, apply joint compound to one side [2] of corner bead.

2. Apply compound to other side [4] of corner bead.

3. While holding knife at 45 degree to 60 degree angle, remove excess compound.

   ● Surface of remaining compound must be smooth and even between panel and end [3] of corner bead.

   ● Layer of compound is approximately 4 inches wide.

   ● Edges of layer are feathered into panel smoothly and evenly so that no ridges or roughness can be seen or felt.

4. Allow to dry 24 hours.

5. Smooth joint by sanding lightly with 220 grit sandpaper.

▶ **Dents**

1. Using 4-inch joint finishing knife, fill dent [1] even with surface of panel.

2. Allow to dry 24 hours.

3. If necessary, smooth surface by sanding lightly with 220 grit sandpaper.

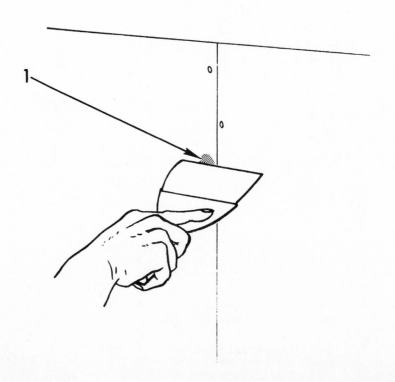

APPLYING THE SECOND COAT

After drying, the first coat [1] will have some shrinkage. Dents and joints can be felt by hand and will be visible.

The second coat [2] continues the process of making the surface smooth and even.

At all joints, edges of second coat must extend 2 inches beyond edges of first coat. Do one side of joint; then do other side of joint.

1. Using 4-inch joint finishing knife, apply compound smoothly and evenly to all joints and dents.

2. Holding knife at 45 degree angle, pull knife firmly over compound to spread compound smoothly and evenly. Remove excess compound.

   - Surface of second coat must be smooth and even.

   - Edges of layer are feathered into panel smoothly so that no ridges or roughness can be seen or felt.

3. Allow to dry 24 hours.
4. Smooth surfaces by sanding lightly with 220 grit sandpaper.

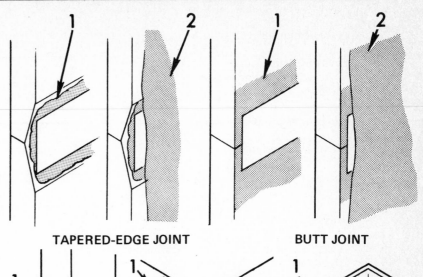

TAPERED-EDGE JOINT   **BUTT JOINT**

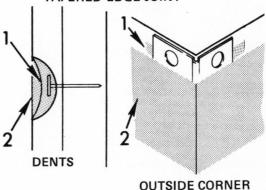

DENTS   **OUTSIDE CORNER**   **INSIDE CORNER**

APPLYING THE THIRD COAT

After drying, the second coat will have some shrinkage. Dents and joints can be felt by hand and will be visible.

The third coat completes the process of making the surface smooth and even.

At all joints except butt joints, edges of third coat extend 2 inches beyond edges of second coat. At butt joints, width of third coat is approximately 18 inches.

Do one side of joint; then do other side of joint.

10-inch joint finishing knife must be used to apply third coat to joints.

Joint compound for third coat may have consistency slightly thinner than peanut butter to aid smoothing.

1. Apply compound [1] smoothly and evenly to all joints and dents.

2. Holding knife at 45 degree angle, pull knife firmly over compound to spread compound smoothly and evenly. Remove excess compound.

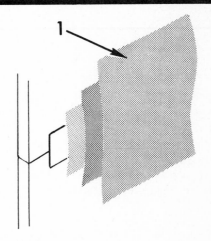

   - Surface of third coat must be smooth and even.

   - Edges of layer are feathered into panel smoothly so that no ridges or roughness can be seen or felt.

3. Allow to dry 24 hours.

4. Smooth surfaces by sanding lightly with 320 grit sandpaper.

83

▶ **Sequence of Finishing**

The following sequence of tasks may not apply exactly to your situation. However, it is applicable to typical construction.

1. Hang doors, if not installed.

2. Texture the ceiling.

If walls are to be papered rather than painted, go to Step 4.

3. Texture the walls.

4. Install molding and trim around windows and doors.

If floor is to be covered with wall-to-wall carpet, go to Step 5.

If floor is to be covered with resilient wood or ceramic covering, go to Step 6.

5. Install baseboards.

6. Paint ceiling, walls and trim, as required.

7. Install cover plates on wall and ceiling fixtures.

8. Install floor covering.

9. Install baseboards, if not installed. Paint baseboards, if required.

10. Paper walls.

▶ **Texturing**

Walls and ceilings may easily be textured with special texture paints manufactured especially for that purpose. They are applied with sprayers, rollers, brushes or sponges to create different decorative effects. Because of the great variety of these coverings, consult your paint dealer for ideas and products suited to your situation.

For the more daring home pro, many interesting effects can be obtained by applying all-purpose joint compound to walls and ceilings. Use brushes, rollers, burlap, sponges or whisk brooms to create different patterns.

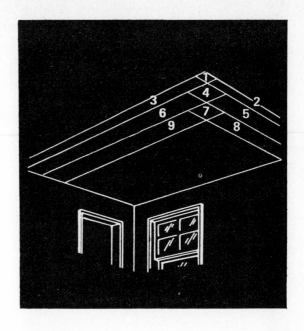

CEILINGS

Ceiling tiles and panels are offered in many different patterns and textures to suit almost any decorating need. In addition, they are available with surface finishes designed for special situations.

Vinyl surfaces which are scrubbable are especially suitable for use in bathrooms or kitchens where moisture or grease is a problem. Other tiles and panels are designed to reduce noise. These acoustical tiles and panels are particularly useful in game rooms or study rooms.

Tiles [1] are designed for application directly to existing ceilings or furring strips. They are commonly made in 12 in. x 12 in. squares or 12 in. x 24 in. rectangles. They are generally constructed with interlocking edges which aid in installation. Procedures for installing a tile ceiling start below.

Panels [2] are used to construct suspended ceilings. They are designed to slip into place in a framework or grid which is suspended from an existing ceiling or ceiling joists. Panels are available in 24 in. x 24 in. squares and 24 in. x 48 in. rectangles.

Suspended ceilings are used in situations where it is desirable to conceal overhead ductwork, pipes and lines but still provide access to them. Access is

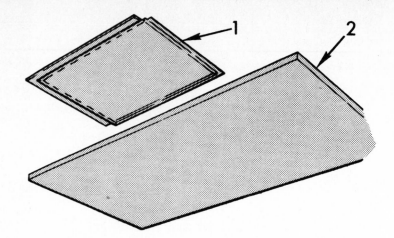

attained by simply lifting and moving aside appropriate panels.

Suspended ceilings are also used to transform a sloped ceiling into a level ceiling.

Finally, suspended ceilings are used in combination with lighting fixtures to create illuminated ceilings. Translucent panels are available which conceal the lighting fixtures and diffuse the light evenly throughout the room. They are often used in kitchen modernization projects. Procedures for constructing a suspended ceiling start on Page 94.

INSTALLING TILE CEILINGS

Tile ceilings may be applied directly to existing ceilings or, if the existing surface is badly damaged, they may be applied to furring strips. Furring strips must be used to provide a level, even installation surface on exposed ceiling joists.

If you have exposed joists, go to Page 91 to install furring strips.

If you plan to apply tiles directly to an existing ceiling, go to next paragraph to check and prepare the surface.

▶ **Checking and Preparing the Ceiling**

1. Check that entire ceiling is sound and securely fastened to joists.

2. Using a 4-foot straightedge, check ceiling for evenness. If ceiling has high spots and low spots, consider installing furring strips to correct this condition. Go to Page 91 for installing furring strips.

3. Check that there are no rough spots or localized high spots. Remove with medium grit sandpaper.

4. Following manufacturer's instructions, mix a solution of trisodium phosphate (T.S.P.). Thoroughly wash entire ceiling.

5. Rinse ceiling with clear water.

▶ **Planning the Job**

The job must be planned thoroughly to provide an accurate estimate of materials and to aid correct installation.

It is your objective to install a ceiling with a symmetrical and balanced appearance. To do this requires that tiles on opposite borders be the same in size. Tiles on border A are the same size as tiles on the opposite border, C; tiles on border B are the same size as tiles on the opposite border, D. If ceiling is irregular [3], make borders on dominant walls [4] equal.

All border tiles must be larger than one-half width or one-half length.

Tiles [1] are positioned correctly. Border tiles are symmetrical and larger than one-half size.

Tiles [2] are positioned incorrectly. Border tiles are symmetrical but less than one-half size.

By moving ceiling tiles [2] one-half of a tile width to the left or right, borders A and C can be made correct. By moving ceiling tiles [2] one-half of a tile length up or down, borders B and D can be made correct.

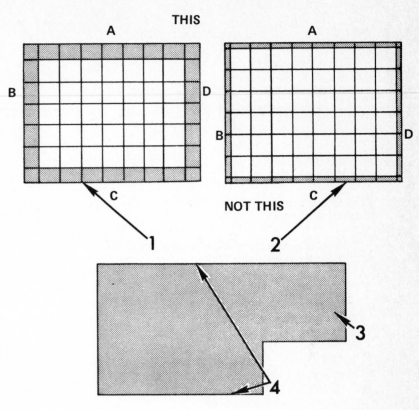

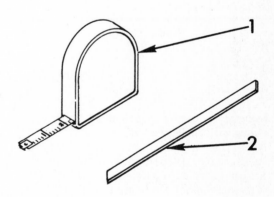

Planning the Job

The following tools and supplies are required:

    Tape measure [1]
    Ruler [2]
    Graph paper
    Pencil

1. Measure and record dimensions of ceiling.

2. Letting each square on graph paper equal 1 foot, draw ceiling. If tiles are larger than 12 in. x 12 in., draw tiles on sketch. Arrange layout until border tiles are:

   ● Same width or length on opposite walls

   ● Equal to or greater than one-half width or length of a tile.

3. Locate and draw all ceiling fixtures and obstructions.

4. Estimate materials in the following manner:

    Tiles — Count number of tiles on sketch. Part tiles count as whole tiles.

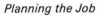

Adhesive — Consult with dealer for product and quantity.

Molding — Molding is sold by the foot. Obtain enough cove molding or quarter round molding to go around entire ceiling. Use dimensions determined in Step 1. Allow extra length for waste from fitting of corners. One or two feet extra should be enough.

Nails — Use 3 penny finishing nails for installing molding.

ATTACHING TILES TO EXISTING CEILING

▶ **Installing Tiles**

The following tools and supplies are required:

    Tape measure [1]
    Utility knife [2]
    Putty knife [3]
    Straightedge [4]. Metal edge is best.
    Chalk line [5]
    Stepladder
    Tiles
    Adhesive
    Molding

Read through entire procedure before beginning installation of tiles.

1. From planning graph, determine width of tile at border along wall [7].

2. Mark ceiling in two places [6, 8] at distance from wall determined in Step 1.

3. Using tack, fasten chalk line to ceiling at one mark.

4. Stretch and hold chalk line tightly between marks [6, 8]. Pull line straight from ceiling and release to mark ceiling.

Installing Tiles

5. From planning graph, determine width of tile at border along wall [2].

6. Mark ceiling in two places [1, 3] at distance from wall determined in Step 5.

7. Using procedures in Steps 3 and 4, mark ceiling with chalk line [5].

Angle between lines [4, 5] must be 90 degrees so that tiles can be installed correctly. Because walls are not always constructed to meet at exactly 90 degrees, angle must be checked. Check angle as follows:

8. Place mark [10] on one line 3 feet from intersection [6] of lines.

9. Place mark [9] on other line 4 feet from intersection [6] of lines.

If distance between marks [9, 10] is 5 feet, angle is 90 degrees. Go to **Page 89**.

If distance between marks [9, 10] is less than 5 feet, angle is too small. Go to Step 10.

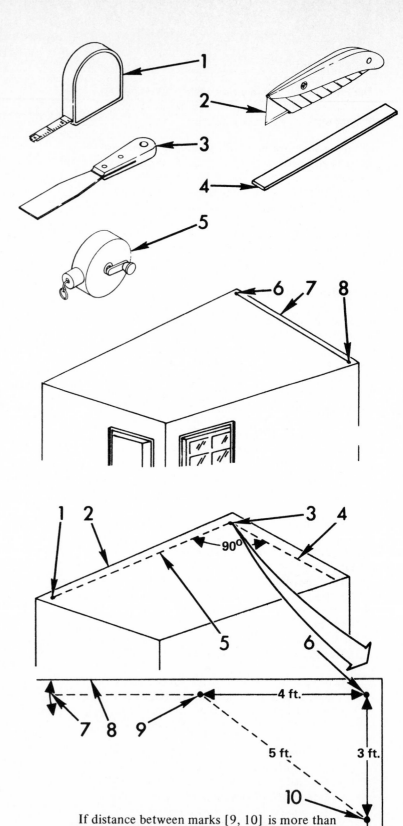

If distance between marks [9, 10] is more than 5 feet, angle is too large. Go to Step 10.

10. Move end [7] of chalk line toward or away from wall [8] until distance between marks [9, 10] is 5 feet. Mark new line on ceiling.

Installing Tiles

Tiles are installed in sequence shown in illustration. Start at one corner [1] of ceiling and work toward opposite corner [4] in following pattern:

- Install corner tile 1; install adjoining rows 2 and 3.

- Install corner tile 4; install adjoining rows 5 and 6. Continue pattern.

When cutting tile, place tile face up. Cut through tile with several light strokes rather than single heavy stroke.

11. Mark tile with dimensions of corner [1]. Be sure that widest (stapling) edges [2] remain on piece [3] to be installed.

12. Using sharp knife and straightedge, cut piece [3] to fit corner [1].

Adhesive [5] is applied in mounds approximately the size of half a golf ball.

13. Using putty knife, apply adhesive [5] on underside of piece [3] near each corner.

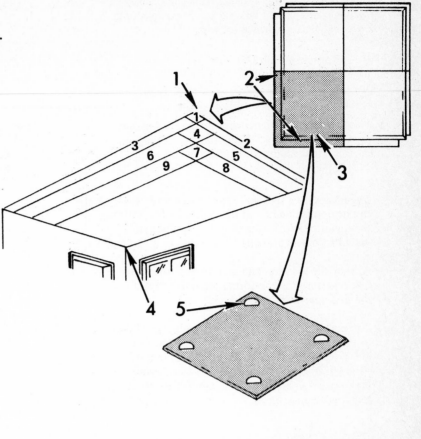

Installing Tiles

Edges [2, 3] of tile [1] must be carefully aligned with lines [4, 6] to ensure that remaining tiles are installed straight.

14. Place and hold tile [1] lightly against ceiling approximately 1-1/2 inches from installed position [5].

15. Using gradually increasing pressure, slide tile [1] into installed position [5].

16. Check that tile [1] is level, and that tile is even with surrounding tiles.

If tile [1] is level and even, go to Step 17.

If tile [1] is not level or even, adjust as follows:

The thickness of adhesive must be increased or decreased to make tile [1] level and even with surrounding tiles.

If adhesive is too thick, press tile [1] evenly over entire surface to spread adhesive.

If adhesive is too thin, carefully remove tile [1]. Add more adhesive and check that tile is level and even.

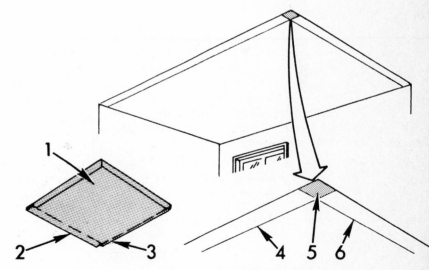

17. Install remaining tiles. Border tiles should be cut and fitted individually.

After installation of tiles is completed, install molding. Go to Page 2 for discussion of molding and installation procedures.

It is a good idea to stain or paint molding before installing it to avoid marking ceiling.

If an existing ceiling is badly damaged or uneven, furring strips should be used to provide a sound, even installation surface for tiles.

If joists are exposed, furring strips are required to provide an installation surface for tiles.

▶ **Planning the Job**

Planning the job begins with preparing a detailed layout of the ceiling. Using the instructions on Page 87, make a drawing of the layout of the ceiling tiles.

The location of tiles and the size of border tiles can be determined from the drawing. In addition, the quantity of tiles and molding can be estimated from the drawing.

So that the location and quantity of furring strips can be determined, information must be added to the drawing.

Furring strips [2] must be installed perpendicular to the ceiling joists [1]. They are nailed to the joists. Therefore, if the ceiling joists are not exposed, it will first be necessary to determine their direction and location. Go to Page 91 to locate and mark joists.

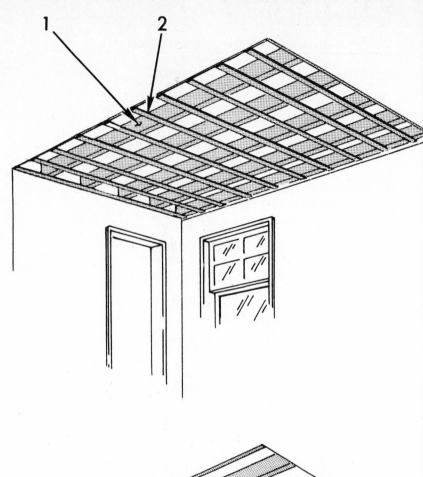

Planning the Job

1. Determine direction of joists [1].

2. Mark drawing of tile layout to show direction [2] of joists.

Furring strips are installed perpendicular to joists. They are located at both sides [3] of room and at each seam [4] between rows of tiles.

Ends of furring strips must be supported by joists. Therefore, allow for waste if exact lengths of furring strips cannot be purchased.

3. Estimate number of feet of furring strips required. Obtain following supplies:

    ●   1 in. x 3 in. or 1 in. x 4 in. furring strips should be obtained.

    ●   Common nails. Two nails are required to fasten furring strip to each joist. Nails must be long enough to go through furring strip, through wall covering and 1 inch into joist. May require 8 penny nails.

    ●   Shingles. Shingles are used to shim furring strips when leveling them.

4. Go to Page 91 for installing furring strips.

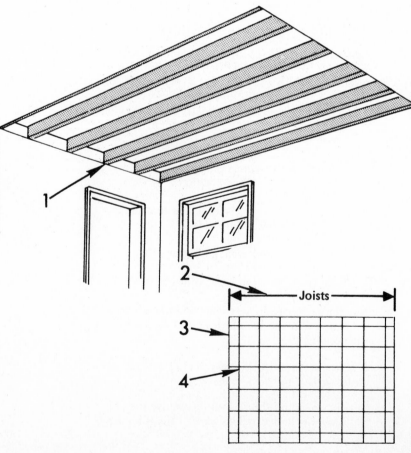

▶ **Locating and Marking Joists**

Joists [1] are often spaced 16 inches apart. However, they may be spaced at 20-inch or 24-inch intervals.

Joists [1] can be located by one of the following methods:

● Nail or drill method: Drive a nail or use a drill and bit to make small holes in ceiling. When nail or bit hits wood, joist [1] is behind surface.

● Magnetic stud finder method: Move magnetic stud finder along ceiling surface until needle on stud finder indicates that joist [1] is behind surface.

Marks [2, 3] must be placed at each end of joist, 2 inches from each wall. Marks must be placed as close as possible to the center of each joist.

1. Place marks [2, 3] to indicate center of joist [1].

2. Place a tack securely at mark [2]. Attach end of chalk line to tack.

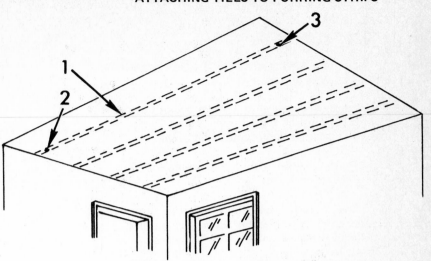

3. Pull chalk line tightly between tack and mark [3].

4. While holding chalk line tightly between tack and mark [3], pull chalk line straight down from ceiling. Release line to make mark.

5. Repeat Steps 1 through 4 to mark positions of remaining ceiling joists.

6. Go to Page 92 (top).

▶ **Installing Furring Strips**

The following tools and supplies are required:

    Tape measure [1]
    Carpenter's level [2]
    Hammer [3]
    Saw [4]
    Stepladder
    Furring strips
    Shingles
    Common nails

Before installing furring strips, be sure to consider the following:

● Furring strips will extend new ceiling down into room.

● Electrical fixtures, as well as any heating and ventilation fixture, may have to be modified to fit new ceiling.

Joists [5], if hidden behind existing ceiling, must be located and marked before continuing. See preceding section (above).

Molding, if installed around existing ceiling, must be removed before continuing.

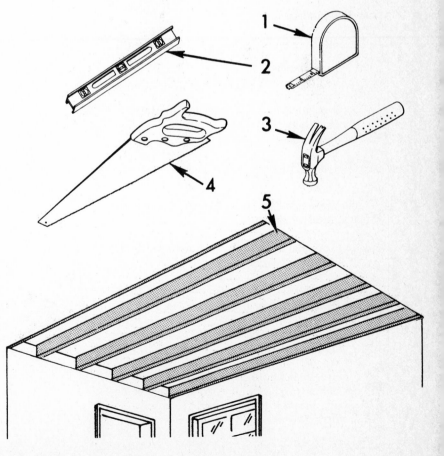

ATTACHING TILES TO FURRING STRIPS

Installing Furring Strips

1. Attach furring strips [1, 3] to ceiling with one one nail at each joist.

Distance between wall and center line of furring strip [2] must be width of border tile. Determine width of border tile from planning graph.

2. Attach furring strip [2] to ceiling with one nail at each joist.

Distance between center lines of furring strips [5] must be width of tile. For 12 in. x 12 in. tiles, distance between center lines is 12 inches.

3. Attach furring strips [5] to ceiling with one nail at each joist.

4. Using carpenter's level, check that furring strips are level. Place shims between furring strips and joists as required to make surface level.

5. Secure furring strips to joists with a second nail. Second nail goes through shims, if installed, to hold them in place.

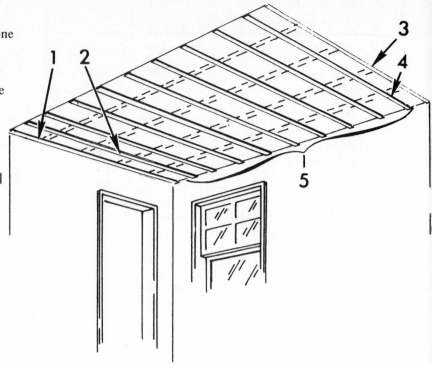

▶ Installing Tiles

The following tools and supplies are required:

    Tape measure [1]
    Utility knife [2]
    Staple gun [3]
    Straightedge [4]. Metal edge is best.
    Chalk line [5]
    Stepladder
    Tiles
    9/16 in. rust-resistant staples
    Molding

Read through entire procedure before beginning installation of tiles.

1. From planning graph, determine width of tile at border along wall [7].

2. Mark furring strips in two places [6, 9] at distance from wall determined in Step 1.

3. Using tack, fasten chalk line to furring strip at one mark.

4. Stretch and hold chalk line tightly between marks [6, 9]. Pull line straight from ceiling and release it to mark line [8] across furring strips.

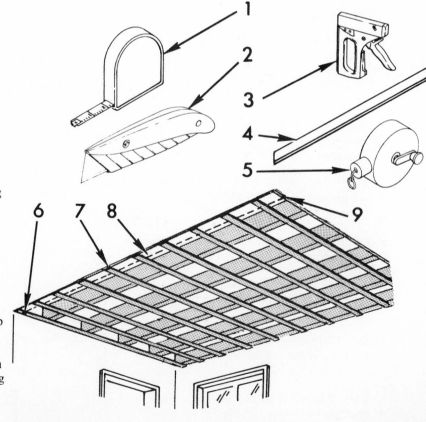

Installing Tiles

Angle between line [1] and wall [2] must be
90 degrees so that tiles can be installed correctly.
Because walls are not always constructed to meet
at exactly 90 degrees, angle must be checked.
Check angle as follows:

5. Place mark [7] on furring strip 3 feet from
    mark [6]. (Marks [6, 7] must be same dis-
    tance from wall.)

6. Place mark [5] on line 4 feet from mark [6].

If distance between marks [5, 7] is 5 feet, angle
is 90 degrees. Go to next section (below).

If distance between marks [5, 7] is less than
5 feet, angle is too small. Go to Step 7.

If distance between marks [5, 7] is more than
5 feet, angle is too large. Go to Step 7.

7. Move end [3] of chalk line toward or away
    from wall [4] until distance between
    marks [5, 7] is 5 feet. Mark new line across
    furring strips.

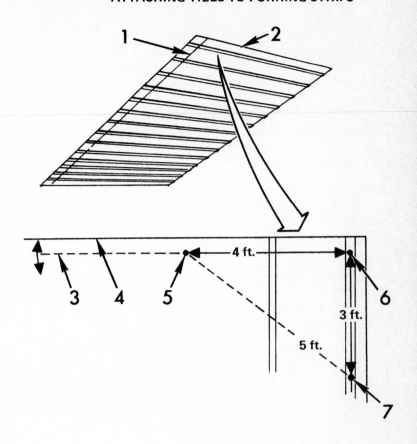

Installing Tiles

Tiles are installed in sequence shown in illustration.
Start at one corner [3] of ceiling and work toward
opposite corner [4] in following pattern:

● Install corner tile 1; install adjoining rows 2
   and 3.

● Install corner tile 4; install adjoining rows 5
   and 6. Continue pattern.

When cutting tile, place tile face up. Cut through
tile with several light strokes rather than single
heavy stroke.

8. Mark tile with dimensions of corner [3].
    Be sure that widest (stapling) edges [2]
    remain on piece [1] to be installed.

9. Using sharp knife and straightedge, cut
    piece [1] to fit corner [3].

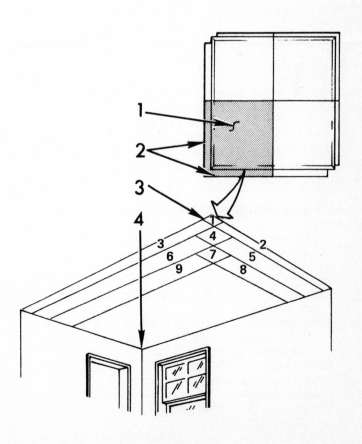

ATTACHING TILES TO FURRING STRIPS

Installing Tiles

Tiles are attached to furring strips with 3 staples in edge [1] running parallel with furring strip and 1 staple in corner of edge [3] running across furring strip.

If tile is at border where access is limited, it will be necessary to attach tile with common nails [1]. Place nails as close to wall as possible so that they can be concealed by molding.

Edge [3] of tile must be carefully aligned with line [4] to ensure that remaining tiles are installed straight.

CAUTION

When attaching tiles, be careful not to damage surface with staple gun or hammer.

10. Using staple gun, attach tile to furring strip.

11. Install remaining tiles. Border tiles should be cut and fitted individually.

After installation of tiles is completed, install molding. Go to Page 2 for discussion of molding and installation procedures.

It is a good idea to stain or paint molding before installing it to avoid marking ceiling.

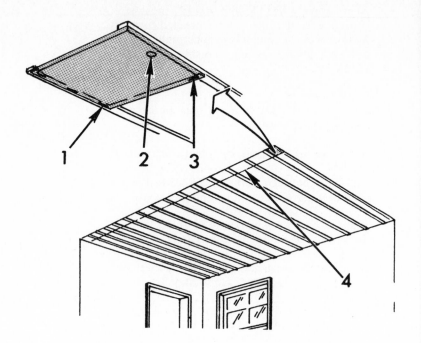

▬ INSTALLING SUSPENDED CEILINGS

▶ **Planning the Job**

The appearance and quality of a finished ceiling depends on how well you plan the job.
Instructions in this section show how to plan and sketch the layout of a suspended ceiling.
The sketch is used to provide an accurate estimate of materials. It is also used as a plan during installation of the ceiling.

The following tools and supplies are required.

Tape measure [1]
Straightedge [2] or ruler
Graph paper
Pencils. Use four or five different colors to help easily identify the different materials you will need.
Main runners [3]. Lightweight metal beams which run perpendicular to the joists. They support panels.
Crosspieces [4]. Lightweight metal beams which connect main runners. They support panels.
Wall molding [5]. Supports runners and crosspieces at wall.
Wire [6]. Supports runners from joists.
Panels [7]

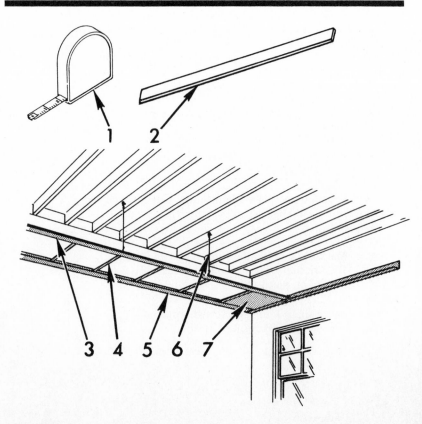

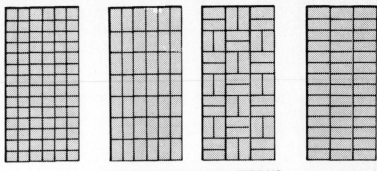

COMMON CEILING PATTERNS

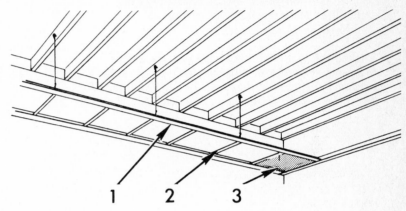

Planning the Job

The pattern of your suspended ceiling must be determined before continuing. The choice of pattern depends entirely on your personal preferences. Several patterns using different panel sizes and arrangements are shown in the illustration.

The pattern determines the arrangement and quantity of main runners [1] and crosspieces [2]. It also determines the sizes of the ceiling panels [3]. Common sizes are 24 in. x 24 in. and 24 in. x 48 in. panels. Select a pattern from those illustrated or design your own pattern.

Planning the Job

On a piece of graph paper, make an outline of the ceiling area to be covered. Most ceiling dimensions can be measured at floor level. Make each square equal 1 foot.

Determine the center lines of the ceiling area. Draw center lines on your sketch.

Main runners are placed with their centers at 4-foot intervals and positioned perpendicular to the ceiling joists. Main runners extend from wall to wall.

If ceiling joists are hidden by an existing ceiling, go to Page 91 to determine their position before continuing. You do not need to mark their position at this time. Indicate direction of joists on sketch.

On your sketch, lightly draw main runners in their planned position. Place first main runner [2] on center line perpendicular to the ceiling joists. Mark other main runners at 4-foot intervals.

The job will look best if borders [1, 3] are at least 1/2 panel wide. If panels along borders [1, 3] are less than half-size, move entire main runner system 1/2 panel to the right or left.

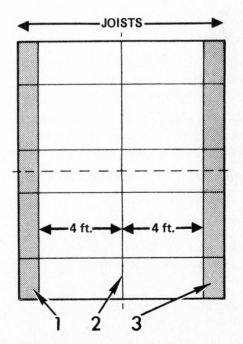

95

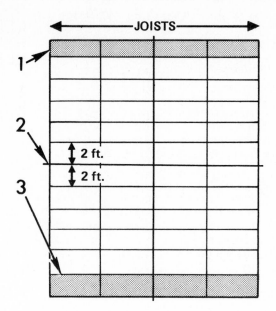

Planning the Job

Crosspieces are placed at 2-foot or 4-foot intervals depending on your planned ceiling pattern.

On your sketch, lightly draw crosspieces in their planned position. Place first crosspieces [2] on center line. Mark remaining crosspieces at 2- or 4-foot intervals.

The job will look best if borders [1, 3] are at least 1/2 panel long. If ceiling panels along borders [1, 3] are less than half-size, move entire crosspiece system 1/2 panel up or down.

Planning the Job

Your sketch should now be a scale layout of the suspended ceiling. Use your sketch to estimate the quantity of materials you need:

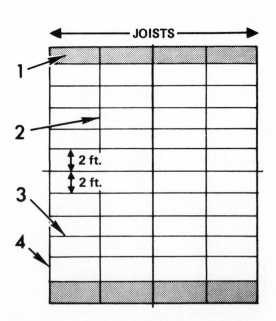

1. Count and record the number of ceiling panels [1]. Account for panels along ceiling border which will require cutting.

2. Determine and record the length in feet of main runners [2].

3. Count and record the number of crosspieces [3]. Crosspieces are usually sold in 2-foot or 4-foot lengths. Determine the quantity of each length required.

4. Determine and record the length in feet of wall molding [4] required around the border of your ceiling.

Planning the Job

5. Hanger wires [1] are installed along the main runner [2] at 4-foot intervals. Determine and record the number of locations where hanger wire is required.

The length of hanger wire [1] needed depends on the distance between your existing ceiling or supports and your planned ceiling height. The next section (below) describes how to select new ceiling height.

If there is any doubt as to type and quantity of materials needed, ask your builder's supply dealers. Be sure to bring your sketch and estimate of materials with you.

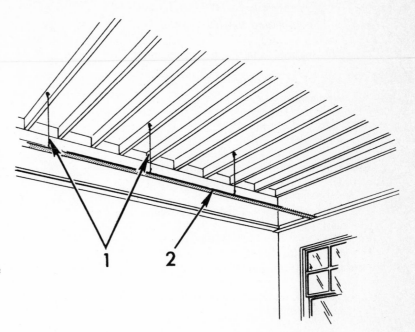

▶ Selecting and Marking New Ceiling Height

When you select the height for your new ceiling, there are several things to keep in mind.

- Allow a minimum of 3 to 4 inches of space [1] above your new ceiling height. This space is needed to allow room for installing the ceiling panels.

- Ceiling height must be above existing windows and doors [2].

- The new ceiling height should be below all duct work, utility piping, and other obstacles.

After selecting your new ceiling height, a line [3] must be marked around the walls to indicate the new height. The line is used as a guide for installing wall molding. Go to Page 98 to mark the new height.

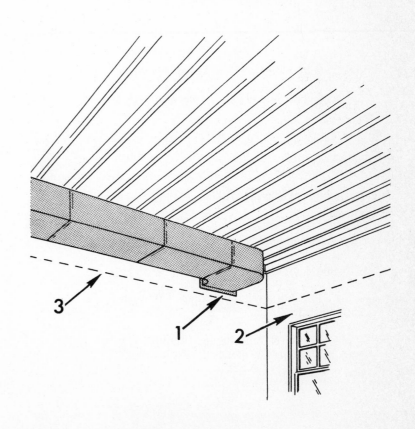

Selecting and Marking New Ceiling Height

The following tools and supplies are required:

    Carpenter's level [1]
    Tape measure [2]
    Chalk line [3]
    Tack
    Stepladder

1.   At one end of wall, place mark [4] at your selected new ceiling height.

2.   Measure and record distance between mark [4] and floor.

3.   At opposite end of wall, place mark [5] at distance from floor measured in Step 2.

4.   Place tack securely at mark [5]. Attach end of chalk line to tack.

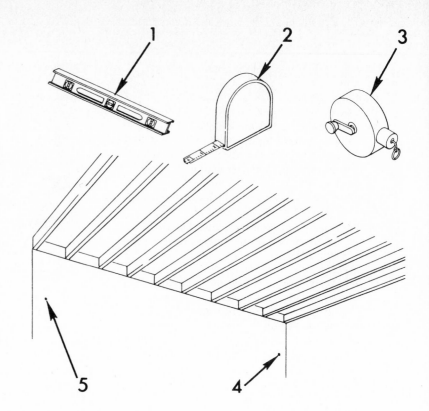

Selecting and Marking New Ceiling Height

5.   Pull chalk line [1] tightly between tack and mark.

6.   While holding chalk line [1] tightly between tack and mark, pull line straight back from wall. Quickly release line.

Chalk line [1] will mark the new ceiling line [2] on wall.

7.   Place and hold carpenter's level against wall and along new ceiling line [2]. Check that line is level.

If line [1] is not level, repeat Steps 1 through 7 until line is level.

If line [1] is level, repeat Steps 1 through 7 to mark new ceiling line along all walls in room.

▶ **Constructing the Grid**

The metal grid system is constructed using your sketch prepared in Planning the Job, Page 94, as a guide. The pattern and dimensions of the sketch must be followed carefully to ensure correct ceiling installation.

Before continuing, new ceiling height must be selected and marked. Page 97.

The following tools and supplies are required to construct the grid:

Carpenter's level [1] to ensure grid is installed level

Tape measure [2] to obtain required dimensions

Hammer [3] and nails to attach wall molding. Nails should be long enough to extend 1 inch into studs for attaching molding to wallboard or plaster walls. For concrete or masonry walls, use concrete nails.

Pliers [4] or common screwdriver [5] to connect main runners and crosspieces

Tin snips [6] or hacksaw [7] to make required cuts

Screw eyes [8] to attach grid system and hanger wires to existing ceiling or joists

Tacks and string to use as a guide for installing main runners

Stepladder

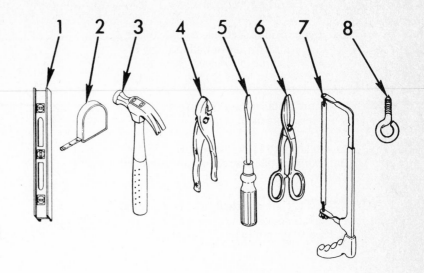

Constructing the Grid

Location of all studs must be known. Page 12.

1. Place marks [1] 2 inches above new ceiling line at position of each wall stud [2].

Wall molding [3] is nailed to wall studs [2]. Bottom edge of molding is aligned with new ceiling line.

When installing wall molding [3] at inside corners, make a straight cut [4]. Molding at corner is overlapped.

At outside corners, make a 45° miter cut [5]. Molding at corner is butted together. All cuts are made with tin snips or hacksaw.

During installation of wall molding [3], use a carpenter's level to ensure that molding is installed level.

2. Place and hold wall molding [3] at installed position. Drive nails through molding and into wall studs [2].

3. Repeat Step 2 until all wall molding is installed.

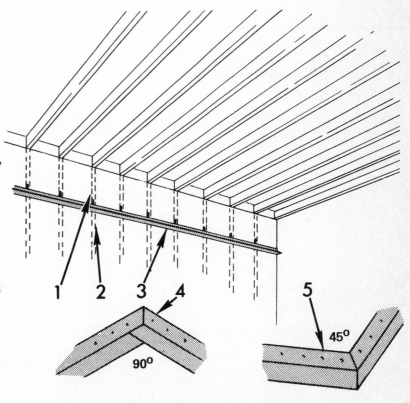

Constructing the Grid

4. Using your ceiling sketch as a guide, place marks [3] directly above wall molding at locations of all main runners. Be sure distance between main runners is 4 feet.

Strings [1] are installed tightly between marks as a guide for installing main runners.

5. Attach strings [1] between marks [3] for all main runners. Be sure strings are stretched tightly.

Hanger wires [2] are attached to ceiling joists at 4-foot intervals above strings [1]. If joists are hidden, Page 91 describes how to locate and mark their position.

6. Using screw eyes, attach hanger wires [2] securely to joists.

7. Pull bottom of each hanger wire [2] as straight as possible to remove slack in wire.

8. Make a 90° bend in each hanger wire [2] at the level of each string [1].

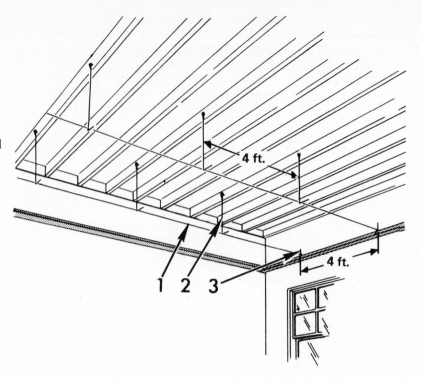

Constructing the Grid

Length of main runners may not be correct to fit across ceiling.

If main runners are too long, they must be cut to fit ceiling. Use tin snips or hacksaw to make all cuts. Be sure that ends of main runners rest on wall molding [5] for support.

If main runners are too short, attach two or more together by inserting end tab [1] of one runner into slot [2] of next runner. Using pliers or screwdriver, secure runners together by bending tab.

9. Raise main runner [3] to height of string. Insert hanger wires [4] through holes in runner.

10. While holding main runner [3] even with string so that both ends of runner rest on wall molding, twist hanger wires [4] securely.

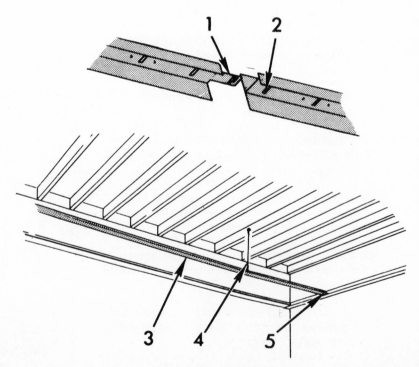

Constructing the Grid

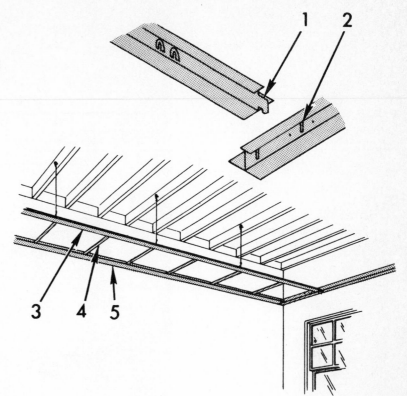

11. Place carpenter's level along main runner [3]. Check that runner is level.

If main runner [3] is not level, adjust height of runner by tightening or loosening wires until level.

12. Repeat Steps 9 through 11 to install remaining main runners.

13. Remove strings.

Crosspieces [4] are installed by fitting tabs [1] on each end into slots [2] in main runners.

Crosspieces along ceiling border rest on wall molding [5]. They may have to be cut to fit. Use tin snips or hacksaw to make all cuts.

14. Using your sketch as a guide, install all crosspieces [4].

15. Install panels. See next section.

▶ **Installing Panels**

Installing ceiling panels is an easy job. Simply tilt each panel up through the grid and allow it to rest between the crosspieces and main runners.

Panels [1] along ceiling borders may have to be cut to fit. Measure and cut each panel separately to adjust for any unevenness along the walls. Border panels rest on the wall molding.

Use a sharp knife and straightedge to cut panels [1]. Panel is cut with finish-side facing up.

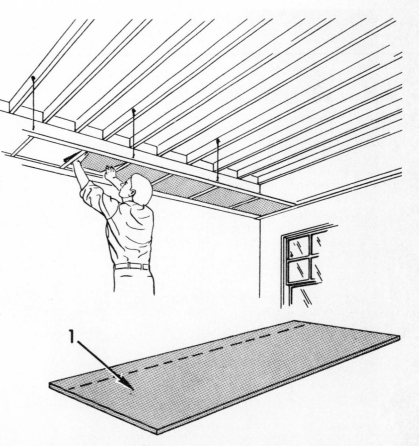

The astonishing variety of ceiling tiles and panels available today creates an alternative to the traditional painted ceiling that is both practical and beautiful.

Typically Victorian pieces in this room include the divan in foreground, gilt-frame photographs, large palms, and the tall parlor cabinet with its glass-domed floral arrangement. The ceiling looks like ornate plaster, but it's actually an acoustical suspended ceiling from Armstrong called "Victoria." *Photo courtesy of Armstrong Cork Company.* (facing page, top)

The tall shelves in this kitchen serve as nesting places for baskets, bowls, and other containers that draw the eye upward to the Armstrong suspended ceiling that realistically simulates wood and plaster. *Photo courtesy of Armstrong Cork Company.* (facing page, bottom)

The clean lines of this contemporary dining room provide the perfect decor for Conwed's textured ceiling tiles. The tiles are produced from inorganic mineral fibers and offer sound absorption, abuse resistance, and a U.L. Class I fire hazard rating. Do-it-yourselfers can apply the tiles with either a staple gun or adhesive. *Photo courtesy of Conwed Corporation.* (above)

Wood parquet-like ceiling called "Stratford" is equally at home in formal rooms like this dining area and in casual rooms like dens. The 2′ x 4′ lay-in panels are actually made of mineral fiber, which has several advantages over real wood, including easy installation and acoustical control. *Photo courtesy of Armstrong Cork Company.* (left)

103

Suspended and tiled ceilings are especially well suited to bathrooms and family rooms.

The versatile "Victoria" ceiling featured in the living room shown on page 102 is equally at home in this lavish bathroom, whose wall and ceiling coverings evoke the Victorian fascination with ornately patterned room surfaces. *Photo courtesy of Armstrong Cork Company.* (facing page, top)

The translucent panels in this ceiling diffuse light evenly throughout the room while concealing the fixtures. The wall planter receives ample light from the ceiling to keep the foliage decoratively healthy. *Photo courtesy of Artcrest Products Company, Inc.* (facing page, bottom)

Old-fashioned ceiling fan and hanging plants give this lush, "busy" room some overhead interest. So does the suspended ceiling, which looks like rough-textured plaster but is actually composed of lightweight 2′ × 2′ acoustical panels. The shiny black grid supporting the panels is recessed for a bold-relief effect. *Photo courtesy of Armstrong Cork Company.* (left)

Lay-in ceiling called "Scotch Pine" has a board-and-plank design to top off the rustic atmosphere of this den. The 2′ × 4′ panels are held up by a lightweight grid which is color-coordinated to blend into the overall design. *Photo courtesy of Armstrong Cork Company.* (below left)

"Lexington" ceiling tiles, embossed with a colonial needlepoint pattern, add just the right amount of flair to the simple harmony of this sitting room. The wood-fiber tiles have a scrubbable Plasticrylic finish. *Photo courtesy of Gold Bond Building Products, a division of National Gypsum.* (below right)